What People Are Saying about *Real Men Don't Text*

Ruthie and Michael bring a fresh perspective to the confusing world of dating. This book is a game changer.

JASON ROMANO, senior manager of social media, ESPN, and former Major League Baseball player

Did you go out last night? Did a guy notice you and ask for your number? Are you now texting back and forth and analyzing each of his words and emoticons? Historically, has this scenario led to a positive and healthy relationship for you? Probably not. So why do you keep doing it?

Turn the page and start reading. *Real Men Don't Text* will shift your perspective. It will ask you tough questions you may not want to answer but need to if you truly desire freedom from unhealthy interactions with men. Ruthie and Michael's words will not ensure you go on lots of dates; they will do something better: ensure you go on the right date with the right guy.

ANDREA, 26, Nashville, TN

In *Real Men Don't Text*, the Deans provide practical and realistic guidance for young women in this digital age. This book is a must-read for all women who are in a relationship or even thinking about dating. *Real Men Don't Text* will change your perspective on how you approach relationships. Ruthie and Michael show you how to be a "forever kind of girl" and help you understand just how much you are worth in the eyes of your Savior.

NATALIE, 18, Anchorage, AK

I just finished reading *Real Men Don't Text* this morning, and it could not have come at a better time. As a college student who has never had a boyfriend, it's been hard for me ~~~~~~ ~~~~ ~~~ such high standards for relationships when I'~~~~~ ~~~~~~~ any positive outcomes. It's also been s~~~~~ text-based flirting and attempts at relatio~~~~

216

and poring over each "Hey, what's up?" late night text from a guy. *Real Men Don't Text* was incredibly encouraging and reminded me that I'm not alone, that it's okay to have high standards, and that the idea that God does have a better love story written for me isn't as outdated and ridiculous as the rest of the word makes it seem.

That being said, *Real Men Don't Text* offers the kind of advice that I want to share with my friends, sorority sisters, and family. It's the kind of advice that's refreshing and doable, especially in a world where dating intentions seem vague and confusing. I finished *Real Men Don't Text* feeling encouraged and hopeful, equipped with real ways to navigate dating in my twenties.

KAITLYN, 20, Gainesville, FL

In the technological world, it's easy to receive and understand the wrong messages. *Real Men Don't Text* gives an accurate picture of the dating world, yet leaves us with practical solutions and *hope*. We all deserve more and don't have to put up with pathetic excuses for dating. Read it! You will walk away empowered and confident!

MAYRA, 24, Monterrey, Mexico

This book is a must-read for anyone who is wondering what they have been doing wrong in their dating life. Follow Ruthie and Michael's advice, and you will be sure to weed out the losers and make the changes necessary to find a real man! If dating is getting too messy and confusing for you, look no further than *Real Men Don't Text*. Ruthie's and Michael's stories are relatable, and we have all been in those places where you are wondering what to do next.

JORDAN, 28, Raleigh-Durham, NC

Ruthie and Michael Dean address the difficulties and struggles of people with lost direction in dating. If you have no clue what your dating future holds, this is the book for you! Maybe you have dating all figured out, but if you don't—read this book! This book helps women end their messy dating lives and start brand-new ones with *hope*. Read and remember.

ZHOU QIU YU, 22, Shanghai, China

Real Men Don't Text is exactly what every woman needs to read to help navigate the current state of the dating world. Ruthie and Michael give a refreshing approach to relationships that empowers us to realize our infinite worth, while speaking truth and grace in a way that any woman can relate. I felt as though I was being counseled by a big sister and brother encouraging me to seek the best for myself in my dating relationships. I believe in Ruthie and Michael's message because their own marriage is a testament that what they are teaching actually works, giving me, and any other woman who reads this book, hope for relationships to come.

KAITLIN, 21, Dallas, TX

Real Men Don't Text is a really great, real book. The pages are full of real stories about real men and women facing the complexities of real relationships in our real world. You'll be wondering how Ruthie and Michael knew exactly what happened between you and your last boyfriend, and the one before that. And the best part—you'll learn about a real God who really knows what love is. The principles in this book really work and will undoubtedly lead you to find a real love. Stop texting and start reading this book! I've already read it three times.

KASSANDRA, 24, Minneapolis, MN

Before I read *Real Men Don't Text*, I thought the men problems I and my sisters have experienced here are just Kenyan men problems, but then I read *Real Men Don't Text* and realized those problems are global. *Real Men Don't Text* is unlike any other dating book I have read because Ruthie and Michael are stating it as it is, making it easy to relate and also embrace the solutions that are offered. Every woman should read this book because this world is not short of men who text to ask you out, or those who feel like they should discuss serious issues like where the relationship is headed via text. It's time for men to go back to being chivalrous, and it's time for ladies to stop encouraging the men problem by texting back. *Real Men Don't Text* is the place to start. It's a game changer!

BOSIBORI, 28, Nairobi, Kenya

A much-needed call to action for single men. Ruthie and Michael do a great job of exposing the problems with passive, meaningless, text-only dating. This book provides clever and relevant encouragement to pursue intentional and healthy, long-lasting relationships.

PETE, 22, Nashville, TN

As a young single doctor who is extremely busy and recently dating, this is the perfect book that reiterates the respect that women deserve and reminds us that *Real Men Don't Text*! I've done a lot of texting, but Ruthie is right: when I like a girl, I will always call. Don't let us guys get away with any more lazy texts.

PAUL, 29, Louisiana

Real Men Don't Text proves "playing it cool" should never take the form of deception or disrespect. Real men date with a purpose and look after the hearts of women who long for a leader to guide them, love them, protect them, and always cherish them.

MARK, 38, Atlanta, GA

We all want to be chosen by someone. This desire can lead us to do some pretty irrational things. *Real Men Don't Text* sends the right message on avoiding these pitfalls and provides guidance for a positive dating life. This is a great book even if you do feel like your dating life is in check. Don't settle—you're worth more than that.

ADAM, 30, Chattanooga, TN

Real Men Don't Text affords women the ability to love yourself enough to not text back. You deserve better! Ladies, do yourself a favor and read this book!

ASHLEY, 31, Nashville, TN

Honest, bold, and to the point, *Real Men Don't Text* is a relevant perspective on dating and underlines the fact that real women shouldn't settle for second best. This is the book for the girls who are in desperate need of hope for their relational baggage and relational future. I'm now happily married because I set standards for my dating life—all of which are described in the pages of *Real Men Don't Text*. A must-read!

SARAH, 31, Huntsville, AL

Though I'm nearly two years into a dating relationship with a man who rarely texts, I constantly see my girlfriends falling into the texting trap. After reading *Real Men Don't Text*, I feel better equipped to encourage my friends to end the cycle and ultimately help them realize that while exchanging witticisms via text certainly feels self-affirming, it's ultimately a cheap facsimile of the affirmation that is offered, not through a man, but through a relationship with Jesus Christ.

CAROLINE, 21, Nashville, TN

Ruthie and Michael have written a book for anyone in a relationship or for anyone desiring to be in a relationship in today's high-paced, social-media-crazed society. They were willing to share and use their own personal life experiences and stories to relate to their readers. It is a book I will recommend to friends, colleagues, or family members that have a desire for a lasting relationship. Thank you, Ruthie and Michael, for your honesty.

MARY BETH, 32, Nashville, TN

Want more confusing, dead-end, text-based relationships? Don't read this book. But if you want to find real love in the time of texting, run to the nearest bookstore or turn on your computer and buy *Real Men Don't Text*. It's about to become the little black book for our generation.

RACHEL, 25, Istanbul, Turkey

real men

don't text

a new approach
to dating

RUTHIE & MICHAEL DEAN

TYNDALE HOUSE PUBLISHERS, INC.
CAROL STREAM, ILLINOIS

Visit Tyndale online at www.tyndale.com.

Visit Ruthie and Michael online at www.ruthiedean.com.

TYNDALE and Tyndale's quill logo are registered trademarks of Tyndale House Publishers, Inc.

Real Men Don't Text: A New Approach to Dating

Designed by Daniel Farrell

Edited by Sarah Rubio

Published in association with the literary agency of Anvil II Management, Ltd.

Library of Congress Cataloging-in-Publication Data

Dean, Ruthie.
    Real men don't text : a new approach to dating / Ruthie & Michael Dean.
        pages cm
    ISBN 978-1-4143-8667-6 (sc)
    1. Man-woman relationships—Religious aspects—Christianity. 2. Dating (Social customs)—Religious aspects—Christianity. I. Title.
    BT705.8.D43 2013
    241'.6765—dc23   2013014072

Printed in the United States of America

19	18	17	16	15	14	13
7	6	5	4	3	2	1

To those who are trying to figure it out just like we are

Contents

Acknowledgments *xiii*

CHAPTER 1 *Real Men Don't Text: A New Approach to Dating 1*

CHAPTER 2 *Real Women Don't Text Back: From the Man's Perspective 15*

CHAPTER 3 *Real Women and Great Sex: Purity Now for Intimacy Later 31*

CHAPTER 4 *Real Men Wait for Sex: More Sex, Better Sex 53*

CHAPTER 5 *Real Women Embrace Beauty: And Tackle the Deeper Issues 63*

CHAPTER 6 *Real Men and the Real You: Finding the Assurance You Are Enough 83*

CHAPTER 7 *Real Red Flags: Run, Baby, Run 91*

CHAPTER 8 *Real Turnoffs: How Not to Attract the Right Man 109*

CHAPTER 9 *Real Women Stop Making Excuses: He's Not Your Last Chance 117*

CHAPTER 10 *Real Men Grow Up: Finding a Man with Direction 135*

CHAPTER 11 *Real Women Give Nice Guys a Chance: Chemistry vs. Connection 145*

CHAPTER 12 *Real Connection: Navigating Relationships . . . Online 165*

CHAPTER 13 *Real Women, Messy Bedrooms, and Hope: When You're Desperate for More 181*

CHAPTER 14 *Real Love: The Story We Didn't Write 207*

About the Authors *223*

Acknowledgments

We would like to first thank Ruthie's blog readers for your incredible support of our writing and this project. Without your kind words and partnership, this project would not have made it past a disappearing blog post.

We'd like to thank Carol Traver, Sarah Rubio, Christy Stroud, April Kimura-Anderson, and Kara Leonino for making this book possible. Thank you for your countless hours and belief in our message. You each brought such unique strengths to the table, and we are honored to work with you.

Steve Green, thank you for making this dream come true. We still can't believe you responded to our initial e-mail (we screamed and jumped for at least ten minutes until we were both hoarse the next day). You have done such incredible work here, and we appreciate your steadiness and reassurance throughout the process. Thank you for freely offering us your incredible wisdom.

Thank you, Sarah Durling, for being the first to suggest this book. Thanks for continuing to press the idea after we skeptically told you there were already too many relationship books. You are such a dear friend!

Thanks to David and Connie Thomas—David, you were the first "real writer" to tell us we were good writers. You both are so dear to us, and we appreciate the sanity you've helped bestow in normalizing our *insanity*. But don't tell anyone else how much we fretted over this book.

Thanks to Natalie Han for being my (Ruthie's) biggest fan. I don't know how many times you reassured me and said, "You are the best writer," but every time it gave me courage to keep writing. We love you, and you'll always have a room at our house.

I (Michael) want to thank the staff at West End Community Church for all your encouragement in the writing process and for being as excited about the release of this book as we are. Thank you for giving me the grace to work and write at the same time!

Thanks to Andy Stanley for preaching such excellent, relevant sermons that inspired much of our advice and gave us the courage to wait and keep waiting despite what the culture encouraged. We would not be where we are today without your consistent wisdom in our lives.

Thank you, Anne Lamott, for writing *Bird by Bird*. I (Ruthie) listened to the audiobook over and over on my distressed runs around Nashville—when I was so desperate to become a writer, but was terrified to take the first step. Your words gave me the courage to stop making excuses and start writing. Thank you.

Thank you, Andrea Lucado, for listening patiently through all my (Ruthie's) verbal processing about this book and for sharing your relationship stories with me. You are such a great friend to both of us.

Thank you to Jordan Dean, Megan Rhinehart, and Christy Wright for reading our first drafts and not telling us we should pursue another passion. Thanks for your hours and edits and kindness. We owe y'all big time!

Thank you, Grace Rhinehart, for reading every single post on the blog and reassuring us we have what it takes to be great writers. Your confidence in us helped us press on.

I (Michael) would like to thank my parents for shaping me into the man I am today, instilling in me integrity, and demonstrating how real relationships should be lived out.

Thanks to Taylor Swift for providing our "writing music"—your songs will always remind us of late nights writing *Real Men Don't Text*. Thanks to Jimmy Fallon for providing humor for our writing breaks. Thank you, Belle Meade Starbucks baristas, for caffeinating our book and for asking about the writing process. Y'all are the best.

Thanks to all the people who shared and believed in this message. We couldn't have done it without your support!

CHAPTER 1

Real Men Don't Text

a new approach to dating

"WANNA GRAB A BURRITO TONIGHT?"

The melody of the Atlanta Symphony's instruments flowed through the auditorium as I stared at his message. I'd been nervously clutching my phone for the past ninety-eight hours. Four days and two hours of uttering the words "call me" into the air. I didn't have high expectations for dating at twenty-three, but a last-minute text containing the word *burrito* wasn't exactly what I had in mind. If you're breathing *and* female, you've been there—waiting for a call, a text, an e-mail, even a tweet—some sign he's still alive. And those are always the days when your mom decides to call you five times and your grandma rings you to ask if you're *still* single. Or, if she's like mine, she calls to *tell* you you're single because you "park with too many fellows."

Mr. Burrito had already taken me on one date, and from my perspective the evening had been perfect—the flowers, the moonlit walk after dinner, the almost kiss at the end of the night . . . the whole shebang. Burritos in an hour didn't quite measure up to that display, but like we all do sometimes, I brushed aside my concern and grasped at any indication he might like me. I wanted to shout, "He loves me!" right in the middle of the symphony, because who doesn't fall in love after experiencing the glory that is a salsa bar? Burritos equaled love in my book.

So there I was, in a swanky black dress and heels, listening to songs from *The Sound of Music*—being summoned by the tap of his thumbs. Did I want to fly out of the symphony and meet him for a burrito? Of course I did. He wouldn't text me if he didn't like me, right? I couldn't remember the last time I'd gone on a date before Daniel, so I needed to take every chance at love that presented itself to me. But did I really want to blow off my family to show up to an establishment where my entrance would be announced by a loud chorus of "Welcome to Moe's!"?

I called my sisters into the lobby right smack in the middle of the rendition of "How Do You Solve a Problem like Maria?" and they graciously—albeit annoyed that my relational drama was keeping them from hearing about the nuns' problem-solving skills—listened to me debate how to respond. The old Ruthie would have texted back and dropped everything to meet him for a burrito. She probably would have kissed him after the date too. I'd had my share of relationships—a generous term for what was actually happening—in which I fully embraced this new path to love in the digital world. I'd respond to texts, Facebook messages, and late-night calls, but it never ended well. I wasted years sitting by a phone, a computer, waiting for men to show me I was worth loving. If only I had known the truth.

Armed with my share of heartbreak, I knew I wanted to try dating differently . . . but did Daniel have to be my first attempt? If I told him I was busy or if I asked him to call, would I miss my chance to date him? Would I scare him away? Would I ruin the chemistry we had? Was it a big deal to meet him for a burrito? Could it be that he wasn't calling me or asking me out in advance because he was intimidated? We always want to be the exception and make excuses for men, don't we?

I took a risk. I told Daniel I couldn't be there on such short notice, but to call me because "I'd love to see you again." Over the next month or two, he texted me he missed me, he texted me to invite me to a party, he texted the weekly "How are you?" message, but I stood strong in asking him to call. We never did have a burrito.

A New Approach to Dating

I had zero guarantees that my love story would turn out well. I envisioned myself sixty and single overhearing friends at parties chuckling with their husbands about how I dated all wrong.

But despite how hard it was to walk away from potential

relationships that felt good now, I set standards for my dating life—because I didn't want several "fun" relationships or a great time on spring break. I didn't want a few weeks of flirty texts and pseudo-connection. I wanted *one* relationship. I resolved to date differently because I learned the hard way that how you date and especially who you date matters. No exceptions.

The truth is, my low self-esteem made it hard for me to believe I even deserved a good man. Could I start over? I didn't know what the future held, but I did know that it was worth a shot to regain my confidence by setting standards for my dating life. I needed to protect myself from jumping into relationships that might keep me from meeting and marrying the right man. Allowing myself to be treated as an afterthought—or worse, a playtoy—bred insecurity and relationships that were doomed to fail. Accordingly, I set basic rules for myself:

- I would not accept dates made over text or social media.
- I would ignore all the late-night calls or texts and decline all last-minute "hangouts" or "dates."

I wanted forever with someone, not just tonight. I soon found a way to weed through the guys who weren't interested in more than a hookup: a simple phone call. It took many single years of imagining myself as a cat lady with my mom remaining my emergency contact, but eventually Michael came into my life and never stopped calling.

"Miss You, Baby"

Safely on the other side of marriage, I started blogging about my not-so-glamorous dating mistakes coupled with small lessons and victories I'd learned along the way. I didn't know if anyone would listen, but as it turned out, there were many women who could relate. My in-box became overloaded with e-mails and comments about heartbreak and confusion and terrible, horrible, no good, very bad relationships.

I heard from women who were frustrated with men who seemed unable to plan ahead. Women who wondered if their dating lives were destined to center around text messages and last-minute "dates." Women enchanted by men who vanished into thin air without a word. A high school student told me her prom date announced his arrival with four letters that popped up on her phone screen: "Here." One woman wrote in and said, "But we talked all the time and hooked up several times—and then he just . . . stopped. I really thought *we* were going somewhere." I heard stories of men announcing their undying affection . . . in a tweet.

Another woman wrote saying she caught her live-in boyfriend cheating on her with a coworker and stayed with her cheating boyfriend because "he promised to change." I heard from women who are in long-term relationships with men who can't seem to muster up the courage to put a ring on their finger. (Eight years—really?) Some of the most heartbreaking e-mails I receive are from women sending boyfriends naked pictures, or sexts, because "it's what everyone does" or "he loves me." I've heard stories of men ending relationships over text, saying "I love you" for the first time over text, and reentering the scene after a long period of silence with something lame like "Out tonight?" or, my personal favorite, "Why haven't I heard from you?" Men are forgoing the former coming-of-age landmarks—mustering up the courage to ask a girl out, walking her to the door, looking in her eyes and engaging her heart—and women are left confused, if not incredibly disappointed.

I don't know your exact story, but I do know that you most likely picked up this book because you have questions about how to find love in the world of texting, Twitter crushes, and online dating. Maybe you are at a place in your life where you can't take one more ounce of heartache and are eager for a new dating strategy. Maybe you just went through a breakup and wonder if texting, sexting, and the instant gratification of it all was the demise of your relationship. Maybe you can't remember the last date you went on and are convinced chivalry is dead. Wherever you are in this confusing dating climate, I want to let you in on the ending of the book before we even get started. Love is not hopeless! In fact, chivalry isn't dead; you just need to put down that phone and set some standards for your dating life—fully embracing the new rules to find love.

"Out Tonight?"

"We wrote letters for two years, and he phoned me and said he'd met another gal."

My grandmother shared with me one chilly Sunday afternoon the story of her first love breaking her heart. Her light-green eyes were surrounded by wrinkles representing years of love—years she'd spent married to my grandfather. She saved the letters from her first beau until she married. Interestingly enough, she and her friends used to sit in parlors discussing a man's intentions based on his *letters*.

For generations men and women have communicated through the written word. Now, we analyze electronic messages. *How long did he take to respond? How many exclamation points did he use? He said he missed you—no way!* "Texting is just how people communicate" is the number one excuse I hear when I challenge women to stop conducting relationships via text. But how's that *normal* communication working out for you? Truth be told, what the culture tells us is "normal" does not *normally* end in a lasting marriage. Advancements in technology have made communication easier, but with this ease comes a shift in relational expectations.

text translation 101

PROFESSOR: MICHAEL DEAN

Him: I MISS YOU!

Her: That's so sweet, LOL.

Him: Why don't I see you out anymore? I miss my girl.

Her: Nothing like a little game of hard to get ;)

Him: Are you busy now? No time like the present, haha.

Her: Haha, umm . . . sure. Where do you want to meet?

Situation: He made out with you last month (or last year) and texts you late at night or just sporadically (possibly after he's been drinking).

Translation: He just wants to make out again. He may like your body, but he isn't interested in knowing you.

Response: Ignore his texts, and if you feel like you can't resist texting back, delete him from your phone book. "I'd appreciate if you stopped texting me" is a great way to gain closure.

Modern communication is not harmful in itself; we just need to be mindful that text messages don't always translate well into relationships.

Have you ever put on your detective hat to read through a string of messages for a friend to determine where the relationship is going? We've all done it. The first "message" Michael sent me was on Facebook. It read: "Hi, Ruthie. It was great to connect with you and hear about all your travels. Keep me updated."

KEEP ME UPDATED?! I read his last sentence at least nine hundred times and copied and pasted his message into an e-mail to ten friends begging them to tell me "WHAT DOES THIS MEAN?"—in all caps, mind you. I remember reviewing over and over that he wrote "Hi, Ruthie" with no exclamation point, which clearly meant he wasn't excited after writing my name—which could only translate that he just wasn't that into me. Or was it that he didn't ever use exclamation points? Or maybe he was trying to downplay his sheer thrill about my *awesomeness*. Trying to figure out men's intentions can make you feel a little nuts.

Let's look at some reasons why you should say no to texting:

- **Texting is easy.** Easy isn't bad; it just means you can't—or shouldn't—start circling dates on your calendar for a summer wedding because he spent three seconds texting you. The thirty-five messages that "blew up your phone" may simply mean he has quick fingers or he likes the attention (more on this from Michael in chapter 2).

- **Texting is not a real connection.** Text-based relationships can bring a false sense of intimacy—the same way following your favorite blogger doesn't mean you actually know him or her. It's easy to feel exhilarated and even connected by rapid-fire, flirty text banter, but text chemistry doesn't hold any weight offscreen. Too many settle for this emotionally addictive buzz in lieu of a real connection.

- **Texting affords both you and him the ability to be someone you're not.** The person on the other end of the message may be completely different than he appears on-screen. You might be wearing text goggles. But just like if you were under the influence of alcohol, you need to take the text goggles off before you imagine he's the one for you. Moreover, lots of men know what women like to hear—"I miss you" or "I wish you were here" messages from a man who is not making intentional dates with you are meaningless. You heard correctly: meaningless.

- **Texting handicaps the communication necessary to build a healthy relationship.** As does social media. Have you ever noticed how people stand around in a class or outside a meeting room and everyone is head down in his or her smartphone? We're losing basic communication skills because we're always plugged in. Had many tough conversations over text or e-mail lately? Yes, it's common to hide hurt feelings and harsh words behind screens. On the other end of the emotional spectrum, Jay Cutler, the quarterback for the Chicago Bears, recently proposed to his girlfriend over text . . . and mailed her a ring(!). Communication is one of the most important aspects in a relationship that withstands the test of time, and carrying out the majority of your relationship over a screen means you are headed for dangerous waters.

Happily Ever After . . . Eventually

What if there is more to this dating hoopla? What if chivalry isn't dead? What if you change the way you date and who you date now to save yourself a great deal of heartache and prepare for an unbelievable future with one man who will make you believe in love all over again? What if you didn't have to spend one more night crying your eyes out or living with regret over your past relationships? You, dear sister, were made for more than messy hookups and disappointing relationships.

I know it's scary to hold men to standards, even small ones like phone calls and planning in advance, because we think these measures will send a great guy running. Even though relationship books for centuries have told us the opposite, isn't there this idea that if we "play it cool" and don't act like "all the other crazy girls" then a man will see we are different, laid back, and we'll live happily ever after? But this casual approach is just a way for men to get what they want without having to commit or really step up to the plate. It's a trick certain men have conjured up to keep us where they want us—available, nondemanding, and easy. I know how it feels to desperately want a man to like you, but if he's not calling, the writing is on the wall: he's just not into you. Setting standards will not scare the right man away, I promise, because men respect women with standards. Let him know up front what you expect and see if he's ready for the privilege—yes, you heard me, *privilege*—of dating you.

You really don't need to spend another minute analyzing his messages and waiting around to see what will happen. If you are unclear about his intentions, simply ask him to stop texting. Ask him to meet the standards you have in order to protect yourself—more discussion to come in later chapters—beginning with a phone call. It's a start in wading through the sea of nonpotentials, the men who don't care to get to know you, because most aren't even willing to call. If you don't set standards for yourself now, it will be easier to give in to texting relationships and compromise in other areas. You will regain days, weeks, perhaps years of your life if you begin to require more from a guy than a lazy message that needs the decoding skills of a Communist spy.

Michael and I share a new perspective on love, sex, and relationships to help you prepare for and find that one relationship we all desire. It's hard to wait for Mr. Right—but you deserve more than pathetic attempts at dating. We accept the kind of love we think we deserve, so in later chapters we'll talk about the "why" behind the tendency to date losers or jerks. We'll discuss how to find your worth, even if you've been told for years that you aren't worth anything. At the end of this book, we can't guarantee you'll meet the man of your dreams, but you will know who you're looking for.

Here's a thought to consider: let's say you started dating

at sixteen. You'll date for six, or maybe ten, or maybe fifteen years or more. But you'll be married for four, five, if not six decades. *Decades.* You may date for one decade. You'd like to be married for five or six. It's tough to feel like you're missing out now by dating differently, but you know what I can guarantee? You will never look back and regret taking *every* relationship seriously. You won't find your husband and wish you had kissed more guys or had more "experiences," whatever that may mean for you. I cannot tell you how many men I let grip my heart, and in turn they squeezed it nearly to death. I'm speaking from a deep well of mistakes, but also from a place of answers. It's never worth throwing away the best years of your life, married to a man of your dreams, because you want to be with someone now.

A year or two after the burrito message, I heard Daniel was engaged. I was still single and wondered if dating differently was a huge mistake. Would I be single forever? But then I noticed something. His fiancée was one of those who frequently posted details of their love story on social media, and I couldn't help but notice he seemed different with her. I just had the sense he wasn't texting her at the last minute or going days without communication. I wondered if he would have strung me along for a few years until he met her—because as Michael will share, if a man really likes a woman, nothing will get in his way.

Another year passed without more than a handful of dates, and then I met my guy. Michael Dean was more than I'd hoped and dreamed to find in a man—what if I had settled? As it turned out, burritos don't equal love after all.

Real Men Don't Text
in 140 Characters or Less

#RealMenDontText

How you date & who you date matters. No exceptions.
#RealMenDontText

If you want forever with someone, not just tonight,
it's time to set standards.
#RealMenDontText

We were made for more than messy hookups
and disappointing relationships.
#RealMenDontText

Dating shouldn't require the decoding skills
of a Communist spy. Ask him to call you.

#RealMenDontText Burritos don't equal love.
#RealMenDontText

CHAPTER 2

Real Women Don't Text Back

from the man's perspective

RECENTLY, RUTHIE AND I were working at Starbucks when a couple, seemingly on a second or third date, sat down. I silenced my headphones as soon as I heard him slam the girl he'd met last weekend, following my intuition that he just might be the perfect example of why Ruthie and I are writing this book.

"I didn't even get this girl's name, so I wrote 'hot b---- with a crooked nose,'" he said, gesturing toward his iPhone. His date listened intently and didn't flinch when he continued to talk about the "random girls" in his phone. He laughed; she laughed awkwardly. She laughed again, twirled her hair, and shifted nervously in her chair, as if she actually liked Mr. Random Numbers. The guy, in Nashville on business, proceeded to hardly make eye contact and not ask her a single question the entire forty-five minutes they were sitting in front of us. I looked at Ruthie, knowing she, too, had silenced her headphones, and she gently shook her head as if she knew what I wanted to do: hand the girl a note that said, "Run!"

I sat there hoping a very large, Nordic-looking guy from the World's Strongest Man contest would come by, grab him by his collar, and shake him out of his Rainbow sandals. *Why would she just sit there? Why is she putting up with this boy who needs a good lesson in dating like a man?*

There has to be something fundamentally wrong in the direction of relationships if these are the kinds of men that women expect. I hear about these situations all the time, but seeing it was an entirely different story. It appeared the woman sitting in front of me was educated, accomplished, and beautiful but had just never learned to navigate her dating life. Maybe she thought he was better than being alone. Maybe they had slept together and she felt guilty and tried to start a relationship. From what I overheard, it was apparent that Mr. Random Numbers had just arrived in Nashville and texted his date, perhaps someone he met on his last trip, in hopes of scoring that evening. After he talked *the entire time*, he asked her to give him a ride back to his hotel. She hesitated, seeming to know what he was really asking, but before I had time to punch him in the face and tell her to read Ruthie's blog, they were gone. It makes me sick that certain men remain boys and that women put up with it. This guy took it to a whole new level. He wasn't just acting like a little boy; he was a fool. And she was allowing it!

The Man You're Dating
MR. TEXT

Olivia and Brian meet at a New Year's Eve party. After flirting most of the night, Brian asks for Olivia's number and texts her before she arrives home. "You home safe? It was amazing meeting you tonight!" Giddy with excitement, she texts back. They go on several dates, and things start to heat up. One night he leans in and kisses her—and they spend the night together. Brian continues to text her over the next several weeks but doesn't go for any of her hints of getting together. Olivia starts to feel desperate. She hasn't seen him since their night together—but wouldn't he stop texting if he didn't like her? Why would he be spending all this time flirting and texting if he had no intentions of seeing her again? She keeps suggesting times to get together, and finally they do, but the next several weeks bring the same emotions. Brian continues to communicate, but he's "too busy" to make time to see her. Olivia is unable to interpret Brian's true intentions because his text messages and actions are contradictory.

Too many women have encountered this guy. It's the relationship that is mostly based on screen conversations—you're never quite sure if he'll come through in real life. It can be elating to drown yourself in endless text flirtations and then devastating when you realize Mr. Text may have no intentions for you at all. This situation is exactly why you need to put down your phone and keep reading. He's telling you how little he values you with his nonchalant communication; you're telling him how little you value yourself by allowing him to string you along.

What Do His Texts Mean?

Ladies, I know how hard it can be to figure out men's intentions. I know how you sit around in circles of friends analyzing our every move, wondering if we like you or conspiring to get us to like you. You make excuses for us and ignore all the clear signals because you want so badly to be chosen. I hate how many of you don't have any clue how much better you deserve as you settle for men who don't care and don't call. You continually make dating more complicated than it needs to be. If he isn't willing to call you after you ask him to, he doesn't like you. And he is not worth your time. If his text messages say one thing ("I love you." "We're soul mates." "Let's get married.") but his actions (he doesn't see you for two weeks, he forgets your dates, he doesn't call) indicate otherwise—he's simply telling you what he thinks you want to hear. He doesn't like you. Over the course of this book, I will help you understand the truth about what messages your guy is really sending—so you can stop the heartache before it starts.

Now, Mr. Random Numbers is an extreme. The thing is, amid the sea of jerks, there are many great guys out there who've just never learned to date intentionally. Many guys haven't had someone teach them how to date, so give them some help and let them know your standards—and see if they are up for the challenge.

I've always been what you would call a "nice guy," primarily because I did have a father who demonstrated for me the proper way to respect and love a woman. But even with the great role model that my dad was, I got myself into some sticky situations by cowardly hiding behind my phone. That's right—texting is cowardly. Men often text because we are afraid of rejection.

Her name was Becca. We were set up on a blind date, and I couldn't take my eyes off her from the moment we met. I was living in Germany at the time (translation: I was lonely) and took any opportunity to date when I came home once a year. We had a good time, but I wasn't sure if I liked her or not. Wanting to find out, I got her number and texted her that night. She replied immediately, and we continued to text incessantly; two days later, I asked her on a second date through a text message—bad move. Within the first ten minutes of our date, I knew clearly that while she was very attractive and sweet, she wasn't the girl for me.

Did I let her know kindly I wasn't interested and make a clean break? Unfortunately not. I continued to text her and respond to her texts because, frankly, it felt good to be liked. I hoped that with each text my feelings for her would grow, but they didn't. However, what I did feel was instant gratification for that part of me that desired connection and wanted to feel like a man. *A hot girl was texting me!* What guy doesn't love that? Plus, I didn't realize I was leading her on. I flew back to Germany and stopped contacting her altogether—no call, no nothing, just stopped. I didn't want to hurt her or have a difficult conversation by telling her straight up I was not interested. I hoped that she would figure it out on her own. A month or two later, she sent me a casual Facebook message and I "didn't want to be a jerk," so I replied. The next time I was home, we grabbed coffee, at her suggestion, because I didn't want to man up and say no, or tell her I didn't have romantic feelings for her. After a year or so of casual Facebook messages, I finally stopped altogether (why didn't someone punch me in the face sooner?). I didn't know or even consider how my actions might affect her.

How would a *real* man have handled the situation? A real man would have picked up the phone after that second date and told her kindly that he would not be pursuing a relationship with her. Instead, I took the easy way out and hid behind vague intentions and messages. I acted like a coward, and I'm one of the "nice" guys.

For men, texting is a sign of laziness and passivity. It's either a tool for players or a crutch for the timid. If a guy doesn't really have to work for something, he won't hesitate to discard it for something even easier. We don't value what we haven't earned.

Our friend Noelle recently met a really nice guy. He had direction in his life and started to pursue a relationship with her, including real dates. She was thrilled!

But then the texting started. At 7:30 p.m. on a Friday he would text, "Want to come watch a movie?" When they were together, he was sweet and showered her with compliments . . . but he didn't seem to be thinking of her much outside of their time together, except for the occasional "I miss you" text or shout-out on Twitter.

For several months, Noelle accepted this as "normal" behavior and just went along with the confusion of their relationship. After all, he had just been promoted (i.e., he was busy) and had just gotten out of a serious relationship. She continued making lists of excuses to her family and friends—"He's shy." "He wants to take things slow." "He is intimidated by me." "He's really busy."—until he slowly disappeared. She felt crushed.

I pulled this guy aside and, man to man, asked him why he treated Noelle the way he did. He expressed shock, as he had no intention of hurting her. I asked if he liked her, and he said, "Of course." But the reality was that while he did like Noelle, he liked the idea of her more. She was a convenient, pretty woman who filled a hole in his life, but he wasn't ready to think about "the future."

Women, most guys aren't out to hurt you—but you can help them by sharing your standards up front. Setting low standards or hanging around until he starts thinking of the future will merely tell him you'll stick around until he finds someone better. You are always teaching people how to treat you. Men won't value or respect you if you don't have respect for yourself and require something better of them.

The Truth about Men and Texting

Does he like me? Are "we" going somewhere? What does his text mean? Here's the part you've been waiting for. It might be hard at first to hear what his texting behavior really means, but this list will hopefully help you remove the wrong men from your life.

- **Mr. Lonely:** He texts you because he's lonely, and you are convenient. He's sporadic in his messages and dates, but can come across as very considerate and genuinely interested. What he's interested in is filling a space in his life, not getting to know you.

- **Mr. Copy + Paster:** Okay, ladies, this might be news to you—but there are men who copy and paste the same message ("Hi! How are you? Plans tonight?") and send it to multiple women. How do you know if you have one of these men on your hands? Start by not responding. If he doesn't text you back until a few weeks later and then tries again—"Hey! Out tonight?"—delay a few hours and then text back, "Yes, but call me tomorrow because I'd love to find another time." If he doesn't call . . . he doesn't like you. Don't shoot the messenger.

- **Mr. Lazy:** He puts forth minimal effort in dating and probably in life, too. He coasts through life and isn't ready for a strong woman like you to challenge him. He may be sweet over text message and may even ask you on a few dates, but they are usually last minute because he can't get it together enough to pursue you. He leaves you hanging for days or weeks between dates. News flash: he likes being lazy more than he likes you. Move on.

- **Mr. Hookup:** He will say whatever it takes to get you in bed. He'll butter you up all week with sweet texts like "Wish you were here"; "Miss you"; "You're the only one for me ;)" when he knows he'll see you at a party on the weekend. Or worse, he'll text you all week, make plans that he never follows through on, and then text you late at night and ask you to come over. Stop responding. He doesn't like you—just your body.

- **Mr. "I Like You":** There is a possibility that the man texting you actually likes you! But listen carefully. A man who likes you or is interested in getting to know you *will* call if you ask him to. That's how you determine if the man texting you is really into you or if he's just looking to fill a void in his life—or worse, in his bed. Texting back, "Hey! I'd love to get together, but I'm kind of old fashioned and only accept dates over the phone" or perhaps "That sounds great! Why don't you call me in ten minutes to talk?" is a great way to quickly figure out if he is genuinely interested.

It is very common for men to collect women's numbers for a "rainy day." We pull out our phones, scroll through the address books, and fish for a response. Your text back validates that we are manly and still have what it takes. Or, we communicate over text message in order to save face, because if you fail to respond, it doesn't feel as much like a rejection as it would over a call or in person.

Some men will tell you exactly what they think you want to hear without meaning a word of it. I don't care if he texted that you're his soul mate, he wants to introduce you to his family, he misses you, he loves you, he can't live without you, he thinks about you constantly, or even that he wants to marry you—if he's not calling you or taking you on dates, he doesn't like you. Stop asking your friends if he does.

A text message can represent a lack of courage and a deterioration of respect for women. We respect standards and love the challenge of dating you. Lowering your standards only perpetuates the cycle because you make it easier for us to drag you along without intention. "Playing it cool" doesn't work because real men don't appreciate *easy*. Easy and convenient might land you a date this weekend, but in most cases it won't get you a ring. You deserve utmost respect and a guy who will commit to you—now start acting like it.

Now, before Verizon or AT&T starts sending me hate mail, a brief disclaimer. I don't have a problem with men texting for a quick change of plans or to say hello during the day. Just be careful to monitor how often you are texting and ask yourself, *Do I feel more comfortable with him over text or face-to-face?* If the answer is text, *you are texting too much*. A great way to escape a texting trap is to delay texting back (one hour is a generally good rule) and then be intentional about ending the conversation. "Okay, looking forward to it! Call me later." As a general rule, texting should always be leading toward a face-to-face relationship, not replacing one.

However, texting is unacceptable for

- the initial "getting to know you" phase of a relationship.
- setting up a date.
- asking you to meet his parents.
- telling you he loves you for the first time.

- arguing with you.
- breaking up with you.
- getting back together with you.

Let me be clear: texting falls somewhere between smoke signals and armpit noises in the chain of effective communication. The truth? If he can't pick up the phone and call you during the first few months of dating, when most men are on their best behavior, how will he treat you down the road—especially if you end up at the altar with a man who didn't have the nerve to call and ask you on a date?

The Man-Boy Problem and How You're Contributing

Texting is evidence of a deeper problem. It's not a phone problem; it's a heart problem. The truth is many men are shirking responsibility when it comes to dating and the general landmarks of adulthood—career, financial stability, and family—until we are left with what you might have heard referred to as the "man-boy problem." I'm sure you know the statistics about women outperforming men and just how hard it can be to land a decent man.

But women are partially to blame for the lack of good men. You perpetuate the man-boy problem by failing to hold the highest standards for yourselves, often starting with the way you allow men to communicate. Men cheat, treat you with disrespect, make last-minute plans, and text you because *you* allow it. You let them get away with all of it. You make excuses because you think going easy on men will perhaps lure them into manning up. The great contradiction is that cutting men slack only decreases their desire to grow up.

Women are spending years putting up with pathetic excuses for dating because they aren't holding men to any standards. Many men don't desire marriage because there's always someone easy who will keep them company on the weekends without the commitment. It's sad how many men and women miss out on one of life's greatest gifts: commitment to one person for a lifetime. Men need to grow up—and the way you can help us is by setting standards for yourself.

A Year without Texts

I want you to consider doing an experiment. Try no romantic texting for a year. Whenever a man asks for your number, tell him up front that you don't text. If you are serious about finding the right relationship and tired of the confusion texting brings, what do you have to lose? Circle the date on your calendar that's a year from now and experiment with dating sans texting. I promise you won't regret it.

If you have let a man know you are interested and he's interested in you, he will call you and even move mountains to see you. Men like fixing, so he will fix the distance between you. He isn't going to wait until Friday evening to shoot you a text about your plans for the night. He won't text you on Thursday at 10 p.m. to ask about your plans for the weekend. He won't text you that he misses you without making plans to see you. He's going to make sure you have plans—because he's called and made them with you.

I don't care what's normal or what your friends allow—by

texting back you are just adding fuel to the problem and setting yourself up for heartbreak. That's right: this is about you. There will be men who won't call you when you ask them to. Congratulations, you've just weeded out another guy who isn't interested in you and saved yourself rejection down the road. If a man can't call to ask you on a date, he's certainly not going to man up enough to put a ring on your finger.

It doesn't matter if he's the most important man on Wall Street or if talking on the phone reminds him of his terrible mother. I don't care if he is shy and hates talking on the phone or if you do too. It doesn't have to be a long conversation—he just needs to exert a little effort to have the privilege of taking you on a date. Don't make excuses for him, because a relationship built on excuses will never last—and will set you up for failure with the next guy. Simply tell him you would love to see him again, but you only go on dates made in advance over

text translation 101

PROFESSOR: MICHAEL DEAN

Him: I haven't seen you in like forever!

Him: I'm so sorry!

Her: It's totally okay, I understand! How's life?

Him: I promise it won't be this crazy anymore.

Him: Let's get together soon ;)

Her: Great!

Situation: He is charming over text, and the relationship gets physical fast, but then he vanishes from your life. He reenters with grand apologies and promises to do better.

Translation: He's only after one thing. He doesn't like you—he just doesn't have the courage to tell you he already got what he was after.

Response: Do not respond. Delete him from your phone contacts. What is he doing in there, anyway? You deserve better!

27

the phone. You might never hear from him again, but then at least you saved yourself a lot of wasted time—time when you could be dating Mr. Right. It's time to stop responding to his text messages and start preparing yourself to meet Mr. Right.

Aren't you tired of putting up with texts and feeble attempts at dating? Sure, there will always be the temptation to go over to a guy's house and just have some fun, but that isn't what you really want. Listen carefully. On the surface it feels good, but it will numb your desires for your future. You want those desires to be sharp so that at the right time and place you can be ready to tell the jokers no and Mr. Right yes.

You Are Worth It

Many of you struggle to know in your heart that you are worth loving, and Ruthie and I absolutely hate thinking about you tossing and turning, wondering, *Why haven't I been chosen?* We don't take your pain lightly. However, it's what you *do* with the hurt that is pivotal. Filling your time with the wrong men or lowering your standards is only contributing to the problem and leading you down a path toward more heartbreak.

Ladies, men are simple, but you have spent centuries trying to understand us—when our intentions are generally clear. You make endless excuses for our behavior—"He is really busy"; "He is afraid of commitment because of his last relationship"; "He had a hard childhood"; or (my favorite) "He's intimidated." No, no, and no! Stop responding to his messages, stop asking your friends, and keep reading. These excuses are why you continually attract the wrong man. A man will pursue a woman he likes. And it won't be through lazy text messages and assumed dates. If he won't man up and call you, plan ahead, and actually take you on a date, he may want to hang out with you tonight, but his future doesn't include you. Cut him loose and save yourself for the man who does want you in his future. Don't lose hope. There is a good man out there for you.

Real Women Don't Text Back
In 140 Characters or Less

#RealMenDontText

Don't put up with a boy who needs to learn
to date like a man.
#RealMenDontText

Stop making dating more complicated than it needs to
be. If he isn't willing to call, he doesn't like you.
#RealMenDontText

If his text messages say one thing and his actions
indicate another, he doesn't like you. Move on!
#RealMenDontText

Mr. Lazy Texter? Mr. Hookup? Ask them to call you & take
you on a date in the daylight. Stop texting back.
#RealMenDontText

It's easy to blame the state of relationships on men.
But how are you contributing? You're texting back,
aren't you?
#RealMenDontText

CHAPTER 3

Real Women and Great Sex

purity now for intimacy later

"LET'S DROP OFF YOUR COAT in my room," Isaac said, leaning in over the thud of the music.

I knew what he was doing.

The steak dinners, the endless compliments, the lines about wanting to be in a relationship. The problem was, I didn't really care. The way he looked at me and put his hand on the small of my back and whispered in my ear made me feel special, adored even. I had been warned about men like him who were just after one thing, but part of me wanted to believe he did mean all those sweet nothings.

As we walked up the stairs, leaving the intoxicated party behind, I tried to push my thoughts aside. Maybe he wasn't like the other guys I'd dated. Maybe *this* time with *this* man would be different.

He shoved open the door, interrupting another couple in the middle of what looked like a heated breakup. "Sorry, dude," the guy muttered, and the two scurried down the stairs, avoiding eye contact. I tossed my fur-hooded jacket in the pile on the chair in the corner and turned to leave.

"Wait. I want to show you something." He grabbed my arm.

"Okay."

The click of the lock transported me to the past. I remembered spending the night in Ryan's room and the next night showing up to find him with another girl. The memory of John, who pressured me physically even when I said no, came flooding back. I remembered my failed relationships with David and Pete and Sam. I thought back to all the promises I had made myself to never be that stupid girl again. My airway felt like it was closing. I didn't know what Isaac's intentions were for me behind his locked door, but I did know that I didn't want to hang around to find out. I'd fallen for the lines too many times, and my heart and self-worth were too delicate to risk another failed relationship. Feeling utterly forgotten has to be like someone has taken your heart and stomped it into a bloodied mess. I didn't want to have to wait by the phone tomorrow, regret and guilt and feelings of worthlessness strangling my already fragile spirit. *But what if it was different this time?*

Before I could leave, his mouth was on mine. He grabbed the back of my head with both hands.

"No," I said, turning my head away.

"Ruthie, I care about you. You're safe with me," he said

with a somewhat contorted expression. He leaned in to kiss me again, but this time I pushed him away.

I left his room. I hoped I was wrong about him and that he did want a relationship.

But he never called again.

Hookup Culture

As a college freshman, I experienced a coming of age of sorts in regard to the expectations surrounding my romantic life. *Sex and the City* spurred many late-night conversations, huddled on dorm beds with my roommates, about this powerful expression each of us possessed. We learned sex could and should produce screaming orgasms; women could have sex like men; and sex was just physical, as inconsequential as buying a pair of shoes. Virginity was no longer a prized possession, as it was in our mothers' generation; now, sexual prowess was applauded. We all came to the room with different opinions about sex and vastly different experiences. Jessica and Elisa had "gone all the way" with serious boyfriends; Leigh and Mandy had "hooked up" with crushes; and Emily told us about her first kiss—but from her all-too-perfect Prince Charming story, we gathered separately that she was just embarrassed to tell us she'd never been kissed.

Leigh and her high school boyfriend had put off sex until college for reasons she never divulged. The fall of our freshman year, they rented a fancy hotel room and were finally going to take the plunge into the uncharted waters of intimacy. When she returned, I welcomed her with a barrage of questions. After a tense period of silence, she said, "I just cried and cried. I keep asking myself how something that's supposed to be wonderful could make me feel so terrible." Her words stirred something within me that served as a powerful reminder of why I was waiting.

A Shoe That Fits?

Sex was a cultural norm in college, and especially out of college, and it didn't seem anyone was talking about the consequences past tonight. My failed dating experiences made real for me what my favorite speaker, Andy Stanley, said about sex: "Sex isn't for in-love people. It's not for ready people. It's for married people."

Before you write me off as someone completely disconnected from society or slam this book shut, you need to understand I made the decision to wait for sex for many reasons—but namely because I knew how shredded my heart felt after rejection from a guy I'd just made out with; I couldn't imagine how unglued I'd feel if sex was added to the equation. Additionally, I decided to wait for sex because it seemed to wreck a lot of relationships. I'd witnessed sex destroy marriages of those dear to me and wreck my high school friends' reputations—so I was open to hearing a perspective other than "do what feels good" or "just be careful and everything will be okay." I believed what Paul wrote in the book of 1 Corinthians: that sex itself isn't bad; it just complicates things when it isn't in the permanent relationship of marriage. Marriage seemed a long way off, but I made the commitment to wait, because I didn't want to experience the hurt that I saw my friends experiencing when their relationships didn't work out.

My countercultural decision raised not only questions among my new college friends but also doubts of my own. I worried my expectations were too high, as my peers told me the man I was waiting for did not exist. There was always the temptation to have sex when I was in love or when I was "ready" (whatever that meant). I remember one friend saying, "No one is that perfect. No guy waits for marriage, at least not one you would want to marry." I had a serious boyfriend in high school, and even though we were sixteen and seventeen, respectively, I couldn't imagine life tearing us apart (note to high school students: your relationship will probably not last). We were *meant to be*, and I was certain he was the only one for me. He went off to college a year before I did and promptly forgot my existence. Looking back, I can think of several instances where I wanted to go further physically, convinced he would be my husband, but I'm so thankful I didn't give myself to a man who left me when distance separated us and another woman stole his affection.

My parents met each other their freshman year at Vanderbilt University, and part of me expected my charming Mr. Right to be walking the same winding paths under the draping trees. But much to my dismay, I didn't meet my husband in college. I spent four years wrestling with questions about sex, dating, and boundaries; swearing off Christian dating books; and ultimately leaving college hopeful I wouldn't be waiting forever. But I had no guarantees.

Many of my peers and numerous men attempted to

persuade me to reevaluate my commitment. "But he really cares about you. It's safe to have sex with him"; "No guy is going to wait for you—so why would you wait for him? What if he's out living it up and you are here gripping your virginity?"; "You would never buy a shoe before seeing if it fits, right?"; "Sex is just physical, and what happens in college can stay in college"; "Everyone experiments"; "What if you wait and then never get married?"; "Men will never stick around if you aren't giving them sex." I'd be lying if I said I didn't have moments where I was just regurgitating one of my reasons and doubt would sweep over me: *If everyone around me is experimenting with sex, is it really all that harmful?* I would listen to my friends' stories about their thrilling hookups, taking note of the seemingly nonexistent consequences, and wonder if I was taking myself too seriously. *Am I missing out?*

I stumbled through, at times firmly gripping my convictions, but confronting many moments of weakness where they slipped fluidly through my loosened hands. I wanted desperately at times to be wanted, and not be alone. I would grow tired of waiting or "purity" and find a man, flirt with him and raise expectations, and kiss him until he wanted more. As soon as I knew he wanted me deeply, I would flee the scene and feel a moment of triumph followed by enormous guilt.

I won't lie to you: I didn't exactly have guys lined up to date me, in college or out. And sure, some would say I missed out because I spent many nights alone in my bed wondering if my commitment mattered. But—this may come as a shock to you—I didn't wear turtlenecks and shake my head at the mention of alcohol or dancing. I still dressed cute, danced, went on dates, and ate at Wendy's at 2 a.m. (i.e., I was not a nun). It helped to have friends who also wanted to save sex for marriage. If you date differently than others, it's important to find some friends who are like you—to keep you accountable and help you feel less alone. If you are waiting, stand strong! No one ever looks back and says, "You know, my life would be so much better if I'd just slept around more." Waiting for Michael wasn't glamorous, but the pain of men walking away from me because of my commitment is long forgotten. The joy of giving myself to my husband is worth a thousand more guys who never called and nights alone.

What I never realized until much later was that my peers and I didn't actually want sex. Sure, for some it might have felt good, but that's not what we really craved. We wanted to be desired. As women, we focus on the way he looks at us, tells us we're beautiful, and confesses he'll never find another. We don't really want sex; we want to be wanted, even in situations where we don't want to date the man, don't we? Most of the men in your life who seem so important now will be a distant memory in the future. It hurts to be chosen and then discarded—more hurt than I think our hearts can handle without breaking.

Mad Men

I know it hurts. A man you love choosing someone else. Feeling alive with desire, hooking up with a man, and then hearing he isn't interested in a relationship. Breakups. Abandonment. A man who you've spent the best years of your life with walking out the door. Him leaving in the middle of the night when you thought "it meant something." Relationships can bring the deepest joy imaginable, but also heartache so acute you have to remind yourself to breathe.

I don't believe sex is just physical, a moment to be forgotten. Whatever happens in Vegas or on spring break or in his room stays . . . with you. That's why you still have dreams about your ex. That's why you will be with your current boyfriend and have flashbacks to intimate moments with another man. Sex creates a physical and chemical connection that is intended to bind your soul to the other person; it always comes with consequences.

I recently tuned in to *Mad Men* and was enamored with 1960s America. The most surprising difference was the smoking. People smoked in meetings, cars, and doctors' offices. Doctors even smoked while examining patients. I knew it was commonplace, as my grandfather had told me how the military gave the soldiers unlimited "smokes," but seeing it on-screen you just want to say, "Hey! Don't you know that smoking kills you?!" Americans were only beginning to discover that smoking—what they were doing every day and what people were doing all around them—was a danger to their health. It was just a pastime, right?

Then all of a sudden, January 11, 1964, rolls around and the public hears for the first time from the Surgeon General that smoking is a direct cause of lung cancer, heart disease, and emphysema. At the time, 46 percent of Americans smoked cigarettes.

My point is that it's not uncommon for the habits society

The Man You're Dating
MR. PROMISED HE WOULD CALL

Ashley and John meet at a charity event, and after talking with her for most of the evening, he asks for her number. He calls her as they stand beside the bar "just so she has his number and knows who's calling." Ashley remains composed but is ecstatic because it's been years since a decent guy (with a job!) has asked for her number. When they part ways at the end of the night, John says he can't wait to take her out. The next morning—Thursday—Ashley wakes up certain that she will have a date on Saturday. She tells all her coworkers about John and spends three hours online shopping for the perfect outfit. But Friday night comes and goes without so much as a word. Saturday, Ashley meets girlfriends for lunch (all of whom are married—and very eager for Ashley to join the club), and she immediately starts asking what she should do about John. Elizabeth insists that Ashley is "so hot and amazing" that John is probably just taking his time planning the perfect first date. "You know what I bet happened?" Ginny says as everyone leans in. "You said he works for Ernst and Young, right? I bet his boss made him go out of town at the last minute. They are notorious for working their accountants to death this time of year." "Ahas" travel around the table. Lydia suggests, "Why don't you casually send him a text message saying you're going downtown tonight and would love to see him?" No, that's too forward, everyone decides. "What about a text that says, 'Hey, it was great to meet you the other night. Looking forward to seeing you again'?" Erin suggests.

The unfortunate truth is that every relationship book you've ever read has it right: men are straightforward. He has not called or made plans with you because he doesn't want to. It's time to move on, sister, because whatever the reason, he doesn't like you. Sending him a text message will not suddenly remind him what a great girl you are. It will only make you look desperate, even easy. Most decent guys will not want to hurt your feelings or reject you and will often respond to your text messages and possibly end up making plans. But you don't want a man taking you out to dinner or pursuing a relationship with you because he is afraid of hurting your feelings. If he doesn't call when he said he would, delete his number from your phone, cut your losses, and move on!

encourages to be wrecking your future. I'd love for you to carefully consider how the way you conduct a huge part of your dating life might be damaging your emotional and relational health. While everyone may be behaving in a certain way sexually, this sexual norm might be slowly eating away at your emotional and relational health. It's worth considering.

Purity Now for Intimacy Later

Let's look at the positive side of waiting for sex. If you look at the flip side of the truth, the beautiful part of sexual expression is that it *is* physical and by design creates an intimate connection like none other. Andy Stanley says, "Purity paves the way for intimacy." Holding off on sex now creates the greater potential for intimacy with your spouse down the road, because sex is designed to bring closeness—a closeness that stays with you long after the act. It will truly be the deepest connection you ever experience. Sex in the context of marriage is freeing and soul filling. I know it's popular to think married sex is boring or unglamorous because it's neither dangerous nor scandalous, but trusting your body to a man who loves you and promises never to leave you is what you really want. I promise.

It requires more self-control now, but if you take a ten-thousand-foot view of your current situation and wait, knowing you are preparing yourself for a greater connection with your spouse down the road, you will look back and be grateful.

Will you choose purity now for deep, soul-healing intimacy later?

R. E. S. P. E. C. T.

Catherine found herself agreeing to cocktails with an old boyfriend. *It's just a drink,* she insisted to herself, and only later admitted she might have wanted more than just one drink. He didn't have a job and asked her to meet him through the familiar "What are you doing? Want to meet up?" text message. They sat at the bar, and Catherine vied for his attention while he seemed more interested in talking to the bartender. Three drinks later, she could no longer drive home and declared she needed to take a cab. He tried to get her to come home with him, and she considered it. *What's the big deal? It's not like we're going to have sex.* She wanted him to like her, and she knew he was a good kisser. But in a courageous moment of clarity, Catherine turned down his offer and told him she needed to head home. Mr. Sans-Job-Texter first asked her to pick up the tab and then let her stand on the street corner alone to catch a cab. As Catherine tried to flag down a taxi, she came to a very clear realization. *How much would I have to hate myself to have hooked up with him? Why am I doing this to myself?* It became clear to her that her willingness to put up with his games demonstrated a deeper lack of care and respect for herself. Sure, she probably would have enjoyed going home with him . . . but the next morning she would have felt more empty and alone than ever.

As women, we long to be loved, to be chosen, to be desired. I remember times when I didn't even care what happened to me. It felt like a thick coat of darkness hung over my shoulders because I felt worthless. But having sex with him will never give us the intimacy we desire. We will only feel more alone in the morning.

The Morning After

We need to start from the beginning. Have you ever considered how your behavior with men stems from the past? (We'll talk more about this in the coming chapters.) Dear sister, I pray you see that you are not defined by your past but have a bright future with a wonderful man.

I distinctly remember the confession of one of my friends who was often lobbying her "sex isn't a big deal" opinion. After a one-night stand: "I felt so used. He just kept going and going, and I thought it was never going to end." I tried to comfort her the best I knew how and sincerely believed the experience would cause her to alter her course. But she continues to have momentary flings—I wonder if it's simply because she forgets what the morning after feels like. Maybe we wait until the emotions grow distant and our desire to be loved comes to the forefront.

I used to be in what felt like an endless cycle of running to men, thinking they could satisfy, only to discover more loneliness and pain the next day. I turned to men because I simply forgot *they* couldn't satisfy me and *their* love wasn't going to give me value. I think it's easy to forget what the next morning feels like. So write down your emotions. How did you feel? What did you believe about yourself?

When we run to men, the moment of desire stands paramount, and the truth that he will leave in the morning (or eventually) is forgotten. No matter how intoxicating a man's love and desire is, no woman wants to be left. If your friends are anything like mine, after a breakup you all sit around eating ice cream, telling one another what a good-for-nothing _____ he was and how "you deserve better." But doesn't rejection always make us feel we deserve less?

Setting Standards

High school was a bit of a disaster for me. If I wasn't changing outfits in the car (my parents were anti–short skirts) or sneaking out to meet the boyfriend they didn't know existed, I was getting a speeding ticket (ten in high school) or throwing a hotel party for my eighteenth birthday. I want to hide under the couch just thinking about it. In order for you to adequately picture me in high school, I need to tell you what my "signature outfit" was. Try not to throw up on the book that cost you hard-earned money. Cutoff jean skirt, midriff-baring tank top, a conch-shell choker, and usually chunky flip-flops. And in the winter? Same song and dance, just add UGGs and a jacket with a fur hood to the equation.

So one notorious winter night (enter UGGs and fur coat with my getup), I told my parents I was going to my friend Nicole's house. I did go by Nicole's to put on makeup to make my story half true before driving to my boyfriend's place. I had two major problems here: (1) I had just gotten my license and had only driven on the highway a handful of times, and (2) I have the worst sense of direction, and these were the days before GPS. I drove around Atlanta for *three* hours until I was a complete sobbing, directionless mess. I couldn't call my parents and tell them I was in . . . well, I wasn't sure where I was . . . and the guy I was going to see was zero help. I had about forty-three dollars in my wallet, and I decided to find a hotel and spend the night. Now, the problem with forty-three dollars is your options are limited when it comes to hotels. And there it was. A purple sign behind the gas station that said Knights Inn, except the *K* wasn't lit up, so I thought it was called the "nights Inn" with trendy capitalization. I checked in, grabbed pretzels from the vending machine, kicked off my UGGS, did stomach crunches (necessary when every shirt you own shows your stomach), and went to sleep. The room smelled like smoke

text translation 101

PROFESSOR: MICHAEL DEAN

Him: Why haven't I heard from you?

Her: Ah, sorry, I've been busy. Didn't know you were waiting. ;)

Him: Always waiting on a pretty girl.

Her: Really? ;)

(Two weeks later)

Her: So . . . what are you up to this weekend?

Him: Hopefully seeing your pretty face.

Her: ;)

Situation: You go on a few dates, then he disappears from your life, reentering weeks later with a message like, "Why haven't I heard from you?"

Translation: He realizes the weekend is coming. He is lonely and looking for some attention. A man who likes you or wants to get to know you will not sit around waiting for you to contact him. Trust me, when a guy likes you, he won't let the majority of your relationship be over text. He will make sure you have plans and that they're with him.

Response: Don't respond. He'll assume you didn't get the message, and if by some miraculous chance he's actually interested in pursuing you, he will call.

and people talked loudly in the hallways all night; but it didn't matter, because I just needed to sleep.

Another quite different hotel experience was where Michael and I stayed on our anniversary: the Four Seasons. If you haven't been there before, picture high-vaulted ceilings in the lobby, all the staff saying, "Mrs. Dean, how can I serve you today?", big white beds that you could sleep in for days, and room service. The restaurant inside the Four Seasons was quite the contrast to my vending machine pretzels from the Knights Inn. It's the linen tablecloth with a single rose in the center, picturesque views of the city, and servers in white coats who ask you if you want a "still" or "sparkling" kind of experience. Michael and I felt like royalty the night we stayed there, and I couldn't help but think how far I'd come since driving around town to meet a guy and then crashing at the Knights Inn.

The Knights Inn and the Four Seasons provide a helpful analogy as you set values for your dating life. You want to be a Four Seasons girl, not a Knights Inn girl. The Knights Inn fulfills a momentary need, a quick place to sleep that won't put a dent in your wallet, but isn't about creating a lasting impression or memory. You can walk into the Knights Inn without a reservation, rowdy and intoxicated if that's your style—because there aren't any standards for staying there. The only lasting memory you'll have from the Knights Inn is the image of the bathroom or the way the sheets smelled oddly like ketchup and biscuits.

Knights Inn girls attract more men because they don't require much from a man. But Four Seasons girls attract men who are willing to spend valuable time and resources and plan ahead. Four Seasons girls may not have as many men lined up to date them in high school and college, but when men are ready to commit and settle down, Four Seasons girls are chosen first. Men realize that in order to be with Four Seasons women, they have to put in some serious effort and treat them with respect. And the truth is all women are Four Seasons material—it's just a difference in how you allow men to treat you. You deserve to stay at the Four Seasons with a man committed to you for a lifetime.

Holding Four Seasons standards might be a tinge painful as you watch all the men line up to date Miss I-Get-Crazy-When-I'm-Drunk or Miss Call-Me-for-a-Good-Time. You may spend nights wondering if your standards are too high and pondering if it's okay to be a Knights Inn girl in college or just this once. But once you lower your standards for one man, it's easy to lower your standards for the next.

I finally realized that I deserved better than a guy who would let me drive all over Atlanta, and I started setting higher standards for myself. I was tired of the hookup scene and the men who would forget about me. Instead of the "I'm a Good Time" sign I'd been holding, I decided to start holding standards. I still went to parties and danced with men—but they knew I was going home alone at the end of the night. I had all the fun my friends were having, but I woke up without the guilt and shame that is often associated with one-night flings. I didn't make a commitment and stick to it with blind conviction. I took some steps backward, but

I kept moving forward, knowing it was important to give myself grace. Grace to you, too, sister.

It is never too late to change your relational life and alter your future. Don't throw your hands up in the air and say it cannot be done because no one will ever truly cherish you. You have worth—whether you gave your body to a stranger last night or you have never dated before—that no one can take away.

Consider these standards that can help you on your way to becoming the Four Seasons woman you are. This list may look different for you, and I want you to hear that's okay. But you do need to come up with some standards, because as Steve Harvey says, "Men respect standards—get some!"

Four Seasons Standards

- **Your man makes dates with you at least two days in advance.** Planning in advance is a sign of respect and consideration. You are not an afterthought.
- **Your dates are always made through phone calls.** If text messages are the best wooing efforts a man can put forward, then he isn't going to do *any better* down the road. *Please* don't make excuses for him. You deserve better.
- **Your man picks up the check on your first few dates.** Men love to spend money on what they care about—and if they aren't reaching for the bill, they don't care about you.
- **You never consider "Come watch a movie at my house" an acceptable date.** Apartments are for

sleeping; restaurants and parks are for talking and getting to know each other.

- **You don't respond to late-night text messages requesting your presence.** Generally speaking, he doesn't want to see what you are doing—he wants to see you naked.

- **You don't do sleepovers.** Even if you're not having sex. Sleepovers easily turn into moving in together and playing house. There is mystery to a woman who won't sleep over. Keep the mystery alive and let him know you don't sleep over with a man who is not your husband.

- **You don't move in.** Studies show that couples who live together before marriage are more likely to get divorced.[1] Don't give me that line about "We want to see if we're compatible as roommates before we take the plunge." You're giving him all the benefits of marriage without the commitment. Move out and see if he proposes! If he doesn't, then you won't waste one more day with Mr. Wrong.

- **You do not sext.** Don't under any circumstances send a compromising picture of yourself. EVER! Those pictures never get deleted. Don't engage in dirty messaging, either, because those messages can be just as incriminating. If it isn't something you want everyone in your phone book seeing, don't send it. We'll talk more about sexting later.

---

1. If you don't believe me, read the study *First Marriages in the United States: Data From the 2006–2010 National Survey of Family Growth* conducted by the CDC. You can find it here: http://www.cdc.gov/nchs/data/nhsr/nhsr049.pdf.

- **You share very few intimate details of your life until after engagement.** Hold off on sharing your I've-never-told-anyone-this-before stories until after engagement is discussed. It's okay to gradually share more intimate, personal details after you're in a committed relationship, but not before then. Oversharing is dangerous in dating relationships, especially with discussing anything sexual. He does not need to know the details of your sexual history unless he specifically asks *after you are engaged*. You are forgiven for your past and it does not define you.

- **You don't sleep with a man without a wedding ring on your finger.** Keeping your clothes on will ensure he isn't dating you just because he likes seeing you naked (clouded judgment)—and keep his intentions honorable.

I realize the above list may seem like you're signing yourself away to a life devoid of dates and perhaps even fun, but I promise you will take less baggage into marriage. Now, if you've already had sex, this doesn't mean you are doomed to a future of terrible consequences because you didn't wait. Additionally, many of you may have had unwanted sexual experiences that will need to be worked through in marriage, whether or not you waited. I want you to hear me say that waiting doesn't mean sex will be perfect, but it does mean you get a head start in figuring out how true intimacy is designed to work.

It's thrilling to sleep with a man who will be in my bed

for the long haul, who I can trust with my emotions. If the current dating climate is as bleak as it seems, isn't it a good idea to forgo how everyone else is dating and start dating differently? You can have fun without lowering your standards or having sex. What if behaving differently now helped a man fall in love with you? The way you date, who you date, and especially who you are intimate with affects your future.

Write down your standards and tape them to your mirror until you have them memorized. I want you to have a daily reminder of who you are, who you are looking for, and how you are taking steps to respect yourself and in turn ask men to respect you. You'll be surprised how quickly you are able to weed through the texters, obsessive video gamers, and players when you're spending your time vertical instead of horizontal.

A marriage in which you are fully known and fully loved is quite possibly the most beautiful of all relationships. Having sex with a man who promises to want you not just when you are twentysomething and hot, but also when you are thirtysomething and working off your baby weight, fortysomething with sagging areas that didn't used to be there, and sixtysomething when you're all wrinkles—it's such a gift, and I want you to experience this unbelievably fun and exciting adventure. When you're on your honeymoon having sex with a man who promises that if he does leave in the morning, it'll be to bring you breakfast in bed, write me a letter, okay?

I'll be waiting.

Real Women and Great Sex
In 140 Characters or Less

#RealMenDontText

It hurts to be chosen and then discarded—more hurt
than I think our hearts can handle without breaking.
#RealMenDontText

Will you choose purity now for deep,
soul-healing intimacy later?
#RealMenDontText

Avoid the morning-after feeling. You deserve better.
#RealMenDontText

You have worth whether you gave your
body to a stranger last night or you have a
perfect dating track record.
#RealMenDontText

Keeping your clothes on will ensure he isn't dating
you just because he likes seeing you naked.
#cloudedjudgment #RealMenDontText

I'm a Four Seasons girl.
#RealMenDon'tText

CHAPTER 4

Real Men Wait for Sex

more sex, better sex

GROWING UP, many boys learn that sex is a rite of passage—something we all must conquer and experience to become a man. Waiting for sex is looked down upon; promiscuity is rewarded. Unfortunately, lust and pornography use have become normal behavior. Men are swamped with sexual images from a young age, and it is easy to access these images anywhere to satisfy our cravings.

The good news is that not all men are sex-crazed animals trying to get you into bed. Good men—men who aren't solely driven by sex—do exist, but the thing about Mr. Right is he isn't standing on every corner. You need to be patient.

He'll never date me if I don't have sex with him. All men care about is "getting some." I have no hope of finding love if I don't have sex. Sex tonight might lead to a relationship tomorrow.

These are just a few of the common myths that women believe about men and sex. I want to help you intelligently navigate this critical part of your relationships. Chances are you've experienced some sort of emotional pain relating to the physical side of dating. My hope in this chapter is to tell you the truth about men and sex to prevent more unnecessary heartache.

I wish I could talk to the guy in your life and figure out his intentions, but an even clearer way to discern if he really likes you is to—take a deep breath—take sex off the table. Make it clear to the guy that you are not sleeping with him, and see if he still calls, takes you on dates, and seems interested in getting to know you. Many women jump into bed with guys, hoping it will fuel the relationship—or start it—when the only thing that sex does is muddle his intentions. Is he calling you because he wants to get to know you, or does he just want to sleep with you? You'll never know unless you stop giving him physical benefits. If he whines and complains, threatens to break up with you, or never calls or texts again, at least you figured out quickly where his heart is—or isn't. As men, we will always work for what we want. Translation? If he likes you, he won't let a lack of physical benefits deter him from dating you. That's the type of man you want to be with anyway, right?

Ladies, you are worth waiting for. You are worth a man committing to you for life and keeping that commitment.

Lies, Lies, Lies

Here are common lies that some men will feed you to entice you to sleep with them:

- **"If you loved me, you would sleep with me."** If a guy ever says this to you, I want you to take a deep breath and turn it around on him: "If you loved me, you would respect my boundaries." Women, some men will tug on your emotions to get you to go further physically with them. Don't let them make you feel guilty, and don't be afraid to speak up. Use your voice.

- **"I have 'needs,' and sex is one of them."** Sex is not a need. No man has ever died from a lack of sex. He may have ninety-nine needs, but sex ain't one. I survived just fine for twenty-nine years of my life sans sex, and he can too.

- **"I love you."** I hate to be the bearer of bad news, but some guys will tell you they love you just to get sex. He may actually love you, but he may just be trying to have sex with you. Not having sex will help bring clarity to his feelings.

- **"We won't know if we're compatible unless we have sex."** How many people do you know who waited until marriage to have sex and then "weren't compatible" sexually? Sexual compatibility is a myth, because it's based on selfish desires and comparison. You will be sexually compatible with someone you love deeply. That's how it's designed to work.

- **"No one will date you if you aren't willing to 'put out.'"** This is simply not true. More on this in chapter 11, "Real Women Give Nice Guys a Chance." Stop dating jerks and find a nice guy out there who will respect your boundaries and even share the responsibility with you. *He does exist*—you're just dating the wrong guys.

- **"Whatever you do in high school, at the frat house, on spring break—it's just one night."** On the contrary, every sexual decision you make stays with you. Memories of the past remain and come up at the most inconvenient times.
- **"The more you physically engage with me, the more I'm going to like you."** This lie is easy for women to believe. However, I've seen more men enthralled by women who won't give in than by women they are sleeping with. We respect standards.
- **"We really love each other. It's like we're already married."** Just because you are living together does not mean that you are married. Don't let a man use that excuse to keep you in his bed and splitting the bills! In that case you are just a roommate he gets to have sex with. Dream come true for him; probably not the love story you imagined as a little girl.

Am I Allowed to Be Sexy?

I'm guessing some of you might think believing in Jesus or waiting for sex means you have to be frumpy and wear baggy clothes. Not the case! Ruthie and I believe that wherever you stand spiritually, you are allowed to be sexy and beautiful. Don't walk around begging people to look at your body, but also don't be ashamed of how God made you. It's a balance that ultimately starts in your heart. Covering up because you are ashamed is no more holy than letting it all hang out. Attraction is not to be feared. The truth about waiting for sex doesn't mean you have to be undesirable. It doesn't mean sex is bad or dirty. Rather, we encourage saying no to sex *tonight* for more, better sex for a *lifetime*. I love what Brett McKay says on his blog *The Art of Manliness*:

> Married men are having better and more frequent sex than their single buddies who go to clubs each weekend trolling for a woman who is willing to take them home. . . . Married sex is even better than cohabitation sex: 50 percent of married men find their sex life physically and emotionally fulfilling, compared to only 38 percent of cohabiting couples.

Marriage equals more frequent, better sex. Simple.

Speaking of sexy—women, you are never to blame for the lust of men. This "if she just hadn't worn that skirt" mentality blames women for men's desire. It is unfortunately more common than I even suspected. I'm tired of Christian leaders telling women not to wear certain clothes or anything that might make men lust or "stumble"—and unrightfully shaming you for the beautiful bodies God has given you. It is simply not true that men are powerless against tight-fitting clothes or provocative outfits. We are not one-dimensional, sex-obsessed maniacs.

We men need to handle our lust issues ourselves and stop blaming women. Ruthie helped me understand that many women live with a great deal of shame about themselves and fear of causing men to lust—in such a way that it's easy to feel shame over merely existing. Let me be clear: *you* are never,

ever responsible for the lust of a man, regardless of what you wear or don't wear. You need to feel beautiful for who you are and not fearful of being attractive to a man, or even attracting one who wants to have sex with you one day. Sex is not something to be feared, but rather to be enjoyed within the context of marriage. Men and women were made with sexual desire, so that a man and a woman could be joined together in the commitment of marriage. Blaming you for his lust is a cop-out and, quite frankly, cowardly. I'm deeply sorry on behalf of all men that we have made you feel like an object to be used and discarded. Your body was beautifully designed to please one man, and culture has twisted this concept into something unrecognizable.

What Men (Actually) Want

What you need to understand is when a man lusts after a woman, his desire is actually for something deeper than a woman. His desire is for God—a deep longing for significance and acceptance from something higher than himself. G. K. Chesterton said it best: "Every man who knocks on the door of a brothel is looking for God." Lust and pornography are an easy way for a man to feel significant and in control in an out-of-control world. Chances are if you have been blamed for lust, the man who blamed you didn't realize that he didn't actually want sex; his desire was for something greater than himself. The same is true for you—your sexual desire is not an object of shame, but rather something God created you with for a purpose. Many men make sex the object of their affection when it cannot ultimately fulfill.

The Man You're Dating
MR. VANISHING ACT

Sarah and Chad have dated for seven months and even decided to spend the holidays together. Chad is the most genuine, considerate guy Sarah has ever dated, and her friends are all green with envy. They've talked about marriage, about kids, and about moving to New York for his job. Suddenly . . . Chad vanishes into thin air. The texts and dates start to dwindle, and then, poof. No phone call, no text message, nothing. Just gone. After four months of being convinced he's been captured by terrorists, Sarah does her best to move on. And then . . . her phone rings. It's Chad! They talk for hours, and he says he was just scared of getting serious. He apologizes over and over and then asks if they can meet. Within a few days their relationship seems back to normal. Then they sleep together, and Chad repeats the same song and dance.

Unless he was imprisoned in a foreign country, a man who disappears from your life is a coward and was only after one thing. No matter how hard he begs and how many grandiose promises he makes, DO NOT get back together with him.

Tied up in a desire for sex is actually a deeper longing for relationship that can only be found in knowing the One who created you and knows you fully.

Married sex is a beautiful thing that allows you to honestly and openly express your sexual desire to your mate. Marriage doesn't tie you down; on the contrary, it frees you to have better, more fulfilling sex. It gives you a chance to trust your spouse fully and give him a piece of you that only he knows. The experience of sex within the context of marriage is a special place for you and your spouse, where you can be known intimately in the trust and confidence of your marriage. Waiting for the one you marry—or making a steadfast commitment to wait from this point forward—will be one of the most impactful decisions you ever make.

How Far Is Too Far?

This question is a common one to ask about the physical side of a relationship, but maybe it's the wrong question. It's similar to asking, "How close can I drive to the edge of a cliff without falling off? Can I hang the wheels off?" The goal of saving sex for marriage is not to shackle your freedom, but to prepare you for a greater future. I don't want to give you a set of guidelines or rules, because you need to make these decisions for yourself. But it is very important that you have *specific* boundaries, because in my experience vague boundaries lead to specific regrets. Many of Ruthie's blog readers have asked about our boundaries, so I will share what was off limits physically speaking in our dating and engagement.

I was unbelievably attracted to Ruthie, so it was difficult for us to wait for sex, especially after we were engaged. (When I say difficult, I'm talking cold-shower difficult.) We set very clear boundaries early on that made our dating and engagement relatively smooth sailing. Neither of us wish we had pushed the envelope more and gone farther. The two biggest boundaries we had for our physical relationship were (1) no sleepovers and (2) no kissing lying down. We stopped "making out" six months before our wedding because the temptation was growing stronger, and we wanted to save it all for our wedding night. We wanted our first night to be amazing, and I would drive back to my apartment each night with this goal in mind. It was unspeakably worth the wait.

You Are Not Your Past

If you are feeling judged or guilty because you've already had sex, I want you to hear loud and clear that you can make a choice today to wait. The future is not hopeless, and your past does not define you. We'll address this concept in more detail in chapter 13. I challenge you to move out, get out of his bed, and change the course of your life. Don't lose heart. You are not defined by the guys you've been with.

You deserve a man who, instead of using you or taking you to a dirty apartment or leaving you when someone else steals his affection, will wait patiently for you and give you the utmost respect and care you deserve. I promise you won't tell me I've steered you wrong.

Real Men Wait for Sex
In 140 Characters or Less

#RealMenDontText

Good men who aren't solely driven by sex DO exist.
#RealMenDontText

"If you love me, you would sleep with me." Lie #1 men tell about sex.
#RealMenDontText

"Sex isn't a big deal b/c we're basically already married." Lie #7 men tell about sex.
#RealMenDontText

You are never to blame for a man's lust.
#RealMenDontText

Marriage doesn't tie you down; it frees you to have better, more fulfilling sex.
#RealMenDontText

CHAPTER 5

Real Women Embrace Beauty

and tackle the deeper issues

I PULLED UP to the coffee house drive-through window, and the barista handed me my favorite drink in exchange for my credit card.

"Wow. You have gorgeous hair!" I said, noticing her thick, shiny blonde hair that danced around her face. She seemed to ignore the compliment, turning to the machine to swipe my credit card. I sipped my coffee, hoping it would summon my writing muse.

She approached the window, and I noticed her eyes were glossy.

"You made my day." She hesitated. "I just want you to know you made my whole day." Her expression announced her lack of confidence, and I sensed she was in dire need of encouragement.

"Well, you really do have gorgeous hair. Mine is thin, and I've always envied people with thick hair," I said.

She smiled. I wondered how long she'd gone without a compliment.

"Well, have a good day. I hope more people notice your pretty hair." It felt like a strange interaction to have separated by a window.

I drove away, my thoughts about the interaction consuming me. *Oh, sister, I hope you find your worth.*

The truth is the barista did have gorgeous hair, delicate features, and a warm smile. But the way she carried herself announced she did not realize she was attractive. Had no one ever told her she was beautiful? She exuded a lack of regard for herself. Had she given up? I wondered what had happened to her and who had told her she wasn't good enough. I recognized her feeling because I've struggled deeply with beauty myself.

Beauty holds many different connotations for every one of us. For some, it's a comparison battle with other women, feeling like we'll never measure up. Most of us strive and battle to climb a mountain toward beauty, only to realize we can never reach the top. For some, beauty holds deep shame, as it's associated with catcalls, aggressive behavior, and even victimization. Beauty can feel simultaneously like a gift and a curse. Most women I hear from have a love-hate relationship with beauty.

I felt ashamed from a young age for being beautiful—because for me, beauty represented darkness and fear. The first time someone told me I was beautiful, I went to the bathroom and muffled my sobbing—unsure of why those words hurt so deeply. On the surface, I was a short, overweight, far-from-popular middle school girl with no athletic ability.

Then I was a high school girl with an addiction to food. Hiding in my bedroom, I would turn out the lights and gorge myself. It was a vicious cycle of desire, giving in, numbness, and then shame. Oh, the shame was debilitating. I hated myself, desperately at times. I was afraid of beauty.

My conflicted relationship with beauty continued into my early twenties, when I developed an addiction to men's affection. I felt shame about my beauty and my body; I was told I was responsible for men's lust. I believed I was worthless because others had told me I was just a "stumbling block," which felt dehumanizing. Beauty felt like a burden to bear instead of a gift. Have you ever felt like your body was a problem?

When I observe the women around me, I see hurt and high walls barricading their hearts. I see women who have given up on beauty because it hurts too much. Women who send pictures of their naked bodies over text message to earn the affection of a man. Others who numb themselves with alcohol or food or attention to keep from feeling the pain of rejection. Women who give their bodies away freely.

If the statistics are true, one out of three women has lost her right to choose at the hands of abusers and predators—often someone she knows intimately. More than half of us grew up without a father to take us to the eighth grade dance and tell us how beautiful we are. When we stick even one toe into the ocean of magazines, TV, the Internet, Facebook, we are reminded that we'll never measure up. There are no perfect families, no stories of smooth-sailing middle school years; each of us has been told at some period in our lives that we are worth nothing.

I recently went to visit a longtime friend. When she trudged toward me at the airport, I knew something was awry. She was wearing sweatpants and no makeup; her confidence had vanished. After a weekend together, she, near tears, told me how terribly ugly she believed she had become. She couldn't bring herself to go shopping or wear makeup, because she "didn't deserve it." Because of some stressors in her life, she had begun to believe that she was worthless. It wasn't about makeup; it was about her heart.

I believe it's important to act in direct opposition to the lies we hear, so I suggested shopping. She wasn't too keen on the idea and listed excuses, but I can be pretty convincing. "Just one hour," I told her, promising to be by her side the whole time. You may be rolling your eyes, thinking shopping is never the answer. But stay with me. In one triumphant afternoon, we went to the mall and my dear friend, a tad begrudgingly, bought new clothes and got a makeover. And suddenly, her whole countenance changed. She walked out of the salon giggling and skipping like a child. It wasn't that the makeup or the new clothes suddenly made her beautiful—it was that now she actually felt beautiful. She believed she was beautiful. I told her, "I want you to look at yourself every day in the mirror and declare, 'I am beautiful,' whether you believe it or not." She told me I was a weirdo, but a week later she called and told me she'd done it. I knew over time she'd see a beautiful woman in the mirror, instead of seeing the ugly, valueless woman the world had convinced her she was.

Many relationship books will encourage you to be more confident, get in shape, eat healthy, buy a new outfit, and engage in beauty treatments to make yourself more attractive to a man. I don't think you should do any of those things to attract a man, but instead to remind yourself that you are beautiful and deserving. If I go to one more church event and see women sauntering around in frumpy clothes, I will scream. God gave us beautiful bodies, not objects of shame or burdens to bear.

"Oh, I could never wear that," a friend said to me the other day about a pair of coral pants she saw. When I asked why, at first she said she'd look weird and then finally admitted, "I've just never been a pretty girl, so it would feel uncomfortable to dress like that." It honestly breaks my heart to hear that many women feel they will never compare, so they hide in safe little worlds of "not caring" or perhaps addiction to numb their desires. How our culture has lied to you!

A Deeper Problem

Our tendency to date men who don't make an effort for us is merely a symptom of a deeper problem. When we have no concept of our worth, it's easy to date the men who don't call the next day, isn't it? I only know because I've been there myself.

After I graduated from high school, I worked as a waitress for the summer. I was terribly insecure and would dress provocatively because I enjoyed the way the other servers would notice and compliment me. I believed I was only as beautiful as the number of men telling me I was—can you relate? One of my coworkers had a live-in girlfriend, but he would tell me *we* were going to get married. He told me I wasn't like the other girls (I was a "good girl with class," I think he said), and for a moment, with his devilishly handsome smile and charm, I believed him. It felt so good to be wanted. It felt good to be validated. A man's desire touches something deep inside that is quite unexplainable.

Another coworker, Mark, also filled my mind with how different and beautiful I was, which quickly led to "hanging out." Our "dates" centered on meeting up after work (read: 11 p.m.) and going to his not-so-classy apartment for drinks. I remember once I told him I was hungry, and he drove me through the Krystal drive-through and asked me to hand over my wallet. We would kiss at his house, and when he wanted to take things further, I felt a desperate desire to keep him happy so that he wouldn't grow tired of me. He would beg and give me reasons why sex wasn't a big deal. All his compliments and the fear of losing him threatened my conviction, but I held on. Our late-night rendezvous continued for a month, and then he abruptly stopped texting and talking to me. The rejection stung; I thought he liked me. I made out with another guy in the name of "feeling better," but it only made me feel more hollow on the inside.

A few weeks later, Mark finally called. I remember running outside so my mom couldn't hear our conversation. I stood on my tiptoes and twirled my hair, thinking he was about to say he missed me and wanted to see me again. I had to fight back tears after learning he didn't want to see me or even hear how I was doing. All he wanted was his shirt back. I was desperate to be loved and wanted but was lost in how to assuage my deepest longing. His rejection confirmed my deepest fear: I wasn't worth loving.

Never Have I Ever

"Never have I ever only had sex drunk!"

"Never have I ever lost my virginity before I turned thirteen!"

"Never have I ever hooked up with two guys in one night!"

"Never have I ever had sex with a married man!"

High fives, laughter, and cheering echoed in the cabin. We were in the middle of the woods on our sorority pledge retreat, and I will never forget the feeling in my stomach. I knew that the girls who stood up and bragged, while they seemed confident, were hurting, possibly in ways they didn't even understand. A standard game of Never Have I Ever gave me incredible perspective.

Every time a new round started, I would watch those who were still standing. After the laughter and cheering stopped, I saw what seemed to be regret and possibly pain. I knew how they felt. It was funny, but then . . . it wasn't.

After we had exhausted the Never Have I Ever game, we all got plates of pizza and came back to the circle. Our leaders asked each girl to share an experience that had shaped who we were as freshmen in college. While some of the girls had triumphs to share, my heart broke over and over as I listened to four hours of coming-of-age stories.

"My father left when I was twelve. Walked out the door and never came back."

"I tried to tell him to stop, but he wouldn't listen. It was awful, and I still have flashbacks."

"He left me on the side of the road, half-naked and drunk."

"My dad never told me he loved me. He went and started a new family."

Women shared devastating eating disorders, the death of loved ones, abandonment by the people they loved the most, and many stories of abuse. The women who had just minutes before told the "best" promiscuous stories were often the ones dealing with the most horrific nightmares where their right to choose was ripped from their grasp. In that room, the statistics had scars and faces. The walls of the cabin seemed to swell with sadness.

As women, we can buy into the lie that our bodies and hearts are mere objects without value. My sisters believed they were worth deserting, abandoning, and abusing—I could hear it in their trembling voices and see it in their eyes. The stories that had brought cheering and laughter during the game now beckoned sorrow from each of us sitting on the wooden cabin floor. But did anyone connect the dots?

Just as my friends weren't engaging in risky sexual behaviors solely because it was fun or casual, we all do this on some level. We run to men to fix or save us—which only causes more havoc on our hearts.

But why?

We accept the kind of love we think we deserve. The root of our disrespectful treatment of ourselves, unhealthy habits, or tendencies to date the wrong guy is a lack of self-worth—often stemming from a deep wound. When we engage in addictive behavior or give our bodies away too easily—we are always dealing with deeper issues that willpower or not shaving our legs (I'm onto you) or making promises will not fix. We cannot simply cover up the past and expect to heal.

text translation 101

PROFESSOR: MICHAEL DEAN

Him: Hey, how are you? Sorry, work has been crazy!

Her: Hey! Great!

Him: Movie at my place?

Her: What movie?

Him: Whatever you want ;)

Her: Sure!

Situation: He comes on really strong—i.e., lots of texts, e-mails, a couple of great dates—and then he disappears or "gets busy."

Translation: He isn't sure if he likes you. And nine times out of ten, he's probably not going to end up liking you.

Response: You need to text him the following: "I had a lot of fun with you, and I'd like to keep seeing you. But I need some consistency in our dates and communication—because that's a standard I have set for myself. If you are too busy for a relationship right now, I completely understand."

If he is being sporadic in his communication, he is uncertain. You want a guy to be certain he likes you. He probably has good intentions and likes the idea of you two together, but something just isn't clicking. Women, men are never too busy for a relationship, but this message gives him an easy way out. You don't want him making more dates with you because he's afraid of hurting your feelings.

It's exhausting to run faster, try harder, and promise our way to healing when the running leads to a dead end and the promises stand empty. For five years, I tried all kinds of tactics to stop turning to men to satisfy me—I punished myself, asked friends to check up on me, regurgitated truth, and promised over and over to do better. But nothing worked because I didn't have a dating problem—I had a heart problem. Until I delved into my past and my fear of not being worth loving, I was destined to a vicious cycle.

Dear sister, there is more in this life for you than this crushing weight of insecurity. There is freedom. There is peace. And I'm sure you've heard it before, but it's worth repeating: it was not your fault.

Big Thighs

So if you ran into me between the years 1998 and 2011, I can tell you exactly what I was thinking about: my thighs. Anytime I ate something that wasn't spinach or perhaps flaxseed, I would imagine the food curling up, all lumpy and warm, on my dreadful thighs. I've tried every workout, diet, and weight-lifting technique to slim and tone my thighs, but to no avail. When I moved to China, I couldn't speak Chinese, and I imagined everyone—taxi drivers, waitresses, Ping-Pong court monitors—saying to me, "Have you seen your thighs? . . . Because I have!" One time I walked out of a gas station and a man yelled out his car window, "Hey gurl! You suuure been drinking yo' milk," which I could only assume meant all that frozen yogurt I ate freshman year of college went straight to my . . . I can't even type it again. If I had online dated during these years, my inability to keep secrets to myself (see, I was born to be a writer) would have yielded some disclaimer about my thighs. Aren't you exhausted just reading about it?

But everything is different now. I rarely (okay, only once a week) think about my legs. I made a decision a year ago to stop loathing my body—after all, all it ever did was get me where I needed to go. All those trips up and down the basketball court and all that rock climbing and mountain biking and Ultimate Frisbee I did at camp every summer had to merit some degree of kindness. While I was at it—that is, drafting a cease-fire agreement to my thighs—I also decided that whether it was my body or my intelligence or my work ethic, I would do my best to stop chastising myself. Because I learned that what I thought influenced who I became.

I'm guessing you have a few choice words for yourself, whether *gross, unaccomplished, good-for-nothing, unattractive, pathetic, unintelligent,* or something worse. Perhaps you speak harshly to yourself without even realizing it. These words may seem harmless, but in actuality they are poisonous to your self-worth, choking joy out of your life. When we criticize ourselves, we look for confirmation from others that we are what we dread most. A man doesn't ask us out, and we believe it's because we are somehow deeply flawed. *He must have noticed my _____!*

In all seriousness, pay close attention to your thoughts about yourself. Do you like what you see when you look in the mirror? Are you proud of the person you are and the life you have created for yourself? At first, you may not be aware of the negative messages you believe about yourself. Here are some questions you should ask yourself as you begin this journey:

- Do you only feel good about yourself when you are achieving something?
- What do you say about yourself in conversation with others?
- How many times do you think something good about yourself? How many times do you beat yourself up inside?
- Do you push yourself to the point of exhaustion and berate yourself when you mess up?
- Do you avoid mirrors because you hate what you see?
- Do you constantly compare yourself with other women?
- Are you dating a man who treats you like a doormat?

The answers to all these questions might touch the heart of the issue and encourage you down a path toward finding *your* beauty. Speaking kindly to yourself and believing the truth leads to a deeper sense of self-worth, affecting every relationship in your life. You will no longer be shackled to the opinions of others and can live free, knowing you are enough.

If you believe you don't deserve more, you will accept disrespectful, maybe even disgraceful, love. If you believe you are unattractive, have nothing to offer a man, will forever be "the friend," or anything similar, you will act accordingly. Remember, we accept the kind of love we believe we deserve. And our thoughts put us on a path that becomes our life—regardless of intention. What if you made a commitment to start speaking lovingly to yourself? What if we all stopped making war on our bodies and talents and accomplishments and sat back in the goodness of simply embracing who we are? Big, glorious thighs and all.

Are You Worth Loving?

I want to ask you a question that on the surface may seem easy, but it's a question worth wrestling with: Are you worth loving?

The spring of my freshman year in college, I described my feelings after being rejected in my journal:

> So he calls me a bunch of times and wants me to come party in his suite. So I drank and went . . . then basically ended up making out with him. He is such a great kisser—and didn't even try to go further. He kissed me like he loved me.
>
> Today, he didn't talk to me. Didn't e-mail me. Didn't text or call. It hurts—I feel so unloved, unattractive, and used. I hate myself again and again. I want him to call. I want him to want me. I want to fall in love. I want him to love me. . . .

The man I thought hung the moon never did call me. After that night, I saw him a few more times at parties, but he ignored me and flirted with other girls. I was desperate for love and would do almost anything to feel wanted. But making out with him—or any guy, for that matter—only deepened my spite for myself because the feeling was situational. When the attention was present, I felt elated, but when it was absent, it felt like a crash—my worth disappeared with the party.

Your friends are probably like mine in that they combat rejection with sayings like "You deserve better"; "You're too good for him!"; "He's crazy not to like you"—right? But rejection often makes us feel the opposite—like we are unworthy of love and will never be good enough for a man. Because if you have never had a boyfriend or you were broken up with or if your father abandoned you, it must mean you are not worth loving.

But what if that isn't the truth? What if you are beautiful and have an extraordinary amount of life inside you? What if I told you that you are worth loving, not because of what you bring to a relationship, but because you have worth deep inside your being that no one can take away?

If men cannot satisfy, men cannot heal, and men cannot save—we need someone more. We need a greater Savior. Brennan Manning, one of my favorite authors, continually painted the picture that our worth is not defined in the perceptions of others, or our ability to "get it right," but in something greater than ourselves. Listen to what he said in his book *The Ragamuffin Gospel*:

> You may be insecure, inadequate, mistaken, or potbellied. Death, panic, depression, and disillusionment may be near you. But you are not just that. You are accepted. Never confuse your perception of yourself with the mystery that you really are accepted.

Here's the part where I give you permission to skip ahead, because I'm going to talk about faith. But before you do, I want you to hear one truth: despite what you have done or even what you will do, you are accepted. Not the best version of yourself or you clutching a string of promises, but you right now, exactly as you are. Hold on to that reality for me even if you aren't ready for what comes next, okay? It will change everything about your love life.

Brennan shared openly about his forty-year struggle with alcoholism and many of the ways he destroyed his life. But he reiterated again and again that as humans we must find our identity in something greater than ourselves—something that cannot be taken away.

I didn't find the answer until I was very broken over the direction my life was heading in college. Actually, that is an understatement. My life seemed to fall apart. My freshman year at Vanderbilt, I went to the hospital with alcohol poisoning. I finally realized that it wasn't just an "Oops, I didn't eat enough" or "I didn't pay attention to how much I drank"—there was something deeper behind that night. On the exterior, I was just another freshman who partied hard, studied like a maniac, and kissed a few guys. But after the music stopped and I was alone with my thoughts, I was miserable. I felt like someone had scooped out my insides. I started drinking more—and hurting myself in other ways— to try to quiet the volume of my thoughts. For me, it took waking up in a hospital emergency room with a cross doctor shaking his finger in my face to realize something needed to change.

I avoided alcohol thinking that would "fix" me, but to no avail. I didn't just have a drinking problem or a moderation problem. As determined as I was to figure it out without a God I had sworn off, my worth couldn't be pieced back together by even my most valiant efforts. I needed more. I surrendered to the notion we were never meant to walk through all the pain of life alone. Life didn't work without God.

It was hard for me to come to this realization because I always felt condemned by religious people, and I didn't want to dress modestly or kiss dating good-bye. When I was in high school, I told God I would never be a Christian because he allowed such terrible things to happen to me *and* Christians were boring, frumpy, and went to bed at 9 p.m. Would I have to attend prayer meetings and use words like *sanctification, accountability,* and *submission*? Would I need to be educated on issues like predestination and women in church leadership or swear allegiance to some big-name pastor? I loved dancing and alcohol and short skirts and cute guys—how could I ever be a Christian? What I discovered changed everything for me. When you compare who Jesus really is with who Christian culture tells us he is, you might discover the two are quite different. Jesus spent the majority of his time on earth with nobodies and prostitutes and others who were considered outcasts—and he really didn't spend much time around "church people."

The message of Jesus is that everyone has profound worth, and neither sleeping with every man who gives you attention, nor lying, nor hatred of others, nor divorce, nor a failed career—and certainly not poor dating decisions—can take it away. As it turns out, God accepts short skirt–wearing sorority girls just as much as he does missionaries or those who have perfect dating track records. I found the acceptance and purpose my soul was longing for and began a relationship with God. He gave me hope in a hopeless world.

Regardless of where you stand spiritually, the truth is each of us holds intrinsic worth. If you believe what popular culture says, we are merely made up of our accomplishments and relationships—but that feels devastating to me. Then rejection and hookups define us. And all the demons from our past void us of worth. But Jesus declares that you, dear sister, are deeply, thoroughly, and fully worth loving. Not because of your promises to never allow another man to treat you with disrespect or your courage to end a bad relationship—but because of who created you.

You're Doin' All Right

It may take years to work on the deeper issues in your life, but the great news is every day you can make choices that will change the entire trajectory of your life. You can take steps to learn to respect and care for yourself—starting with your thoughts and small actions that display love for yourself, which Michael will detail in the next chapter. Let's change our direction and take steps toward becoming women who live in the knowledge that we are loved. We must redefine beautiful. Beautiful is not a short skirt, a size 2 pair of skinny jeans, or a fresh face of makeup—it is who we are as women. Beautiful is caring for yourself and loving yourself well. Beautiful is taking the steps you need to deal with your past so it does not destroy your future. Beauty is something no man can take away from you.

Sister, you are worth loving, and I hope you start by loving and treating yourself well while you work on the deeper issues in your past. I want you to experience a moment like I did when I decided to stop focusing on my failures and loathing my appearance. One night Michael took me to a fancy hotel, and I went to the gym to pound out a few miles to make my thighs at least feel a little smaller. Unfortunately, it was one of those gyms with a ceiling-length mirror directly in front of the treadmill (incentive to run faster, I suppose). I hated looking at myself in that awful mirror under the fluorescent lights, and thoughts of self-loathing swirled . . . until I couldn't stand it anymore. I jumped off and nearly fell to my knees. After I caught my breath, I looked in the mirror and thought long and hard about who I'd become. Slowly, I smiled. "You're doin' all right," I said, almost in a whisper. I made a truce with my thighs that day, deciding to stop hating them. Instead, I promised to lovingly remember all the beautiful places they have taken me: villages in China, deep creeks in the Georgia woods, and gracefully down the aisle toward my groom.

Real Women Embrace Beauty
In 140 Characters or Less

#RealMenDontText

Has no one ever told you how beautiful you are?
What you are worth? It is time you know.
#RealMenDontText

God gave us beautiful bodies, not objects of shame
or burdens to bear.
#RealMenDontText

We accept the kind of love we think we deserve.
#RealMenDontText

Do you like what you see in the mirror? Learn to love
YOU before you ask a man to love you.
#RealMenDontText

If men cannot satisfy, heal, or save, we need someone
more. We need a greater Savior.
#RealMenDontText

CHAPTER 6

Real Men and the Real You

finding the assurance you are enough

"I FIRST NOTICED my wife because she stood up to a girl who was bashing her boyfriend in front of the group. I saw her heart."

"Nice long legs," he said with a chuckle. "The attraction was physical at first, but then we went out to dinner with a group of friends, and she was just funny and just kind of took charge of the conversations. She was just way out of my league on multiple levels."

"Her down-to-earthness and confidence."

"I thought she was beautiful from the very first time I saw her. Good chemistry from the beginning. Then we started dating, got married, and had a baby. I think she's just as cute as the day I met her."

"Love at first sight."

"She nervous-talked in this overly loud voice and laughed at her own jokes. I knew she was the only one for me!"

I knew every man is attracted to different character and physical qualities in women, so to "prove it" I asked a myriad of different men a simple question: "What first attracted you to your wife?" Did you notice how different the responses were? Over the years, I've noted what vastly dissimilar women my friends and I ended up marrying. We have short and tall, artists and lawyers, thin and curvy, athletes and cooks, introverts and life-of-the-party types. The good news is that every guy has unique tastes when it comes to what woman he fancies. Translation: you have what it takes to attract a good man.

Women, you generally believe that appearance is the first quality men notice, but attraction goes much deeper. If you listen to men talk about first meeting their wives, the phrases "she had me at hello," "she took my breath away," and "I couldn't take my eyes off her" are often mentioned. If you dig further, you usually find words like *selfless*, *caring*, *charming*, *kind*, and descriptions about what great moms or friends their wives are—but these usually come after the initial attraction. Confidence actually makes all the difference when it comes to attraction. Confidence is not a personality. If you are quiet, be quiet. If you are outgoing, be outgoing. Confidence is the quiet assurance you are enough. The assurance that no matter if men are lined up outside your door or no one has ever asked you on a date, you are beautiful.

Here's something I've noticed. Like Ruthie noted, I see women around me who have, in a sense, given up on beauty. Their general lack of regard for their appearance announces to every man in the room that they don't care for themselves. If you have struggled with knowing you are beautiful, I absolutely hate that for you. I can't imagine the pain of not being chosen or feeling like you will never measure up. But if you can't learn to care for and love yourself, how can you expect a man to do so?

I asked Ruthie what she used to believe men were attracted to before we met, and she told me she had ingrained in her mind that "guys like skinny, quiet girls." Hilarious, mainly because my wife could not be quiet if she tried (and try she did). It is no secret that men are visually inclined, but the myth that "no man will like me unless I am a size 2 and have big breasts" is simply false! All this type of thinking does is encourage you to hide your true self—a self that one man will be captivated by. Striving for a stereotype and forcing yourself into a tiny mold of beauty leads to an exhausting dead end.

text translation 101

PROFESSOR: MICHAEL DEAN

Him: Can't stop thinking about last night.

Her: :) What do you mean?

Him: Your body. HOT.

Her: Oh whatever.

Him: Send me a pic?

Him: Come on . . . I'll send you one first? lol

Situation: *He asks you—maybe begs you—for a picture. And you know exactly what kind of picture he's talking about.*

Translation: *He doesn't care about you. He is treating you like an object, and you deserve better.*

Response: *Do not respond.*

You are the best person at being you. Mr. Right is looking for a woman who is confident in who she is and comfortable in her own skin. Working on healing from your past might take years, but I want us to look at some practical ways that you can begin to embrace the beautiful and confident woman you are meant to be. I want to address specifically women who feel that they have never been chosen. I understand it can seem much easier to hide behind extra weight, shabby clothes, or negative self-talk. My hope is that you will finish this chapter with confidence and assurance that you are enough.

Are You Caring for YOU?

Let's dive in. Write down a quote or saying that summarizes your value. Carry it in your purse or stick it on your bathroom mirror. List qualities you love about yourself below this quote to remind you of what you have to offer to a man. Seriously, you have a lot to offer! This exercise might feel awkward, but if you love your dazzling blue eyes—write it down! Your loyalty to friends and family? Write. Your womanly figure? Perfect. This reminder is vital in a world that will always tell you that you are not enough, repeating this lie in every magazine and commercial.

Now it's time for the practical steps toward discovering your worth. The reason it was important for Ruthie's friend to go shopping and put on makeup when she felt terrible about herself was because it was a tangible way of "walking out" the truth. The following list is not to catch a man; rather, think of it as a "self-worth project"—actions to take to ensure you are caring for yourself and instilling confidence.

- **Eating.** Develop healthy eating habits. Carve out time in your day to cook or toss together a salad. Try Weight Watchers if you need to lose weight—I don't know a better program for long-term sustainable weight loss. Spend the extra money you need on healthy foods. If you are an overeater, stop buying foods that are tempting for late-night eating and only keep healthy foods in the house. In the Dean house, we don't keep chips, dessert, or traditional snack foods around because Ruthie would just rather avoid altogether the temptation to "eat her feelings." If you tend to skip meals or punish yourself for missing a workout, learn to love yourself and nourish your body. It's hard work to love ourselves in a culture that seems obsessed with reminding us we'll never measure up— but there are too many wonderful things you'll miss if you are controlled by food and appearance.

- **Exercise.** I know in today's busy world it's hard to find time to do laundry, much less go to the gym. But the reality is that you spend time on what's important to you! And if you can't find time to spend taking care of yourself, then you aren't a high enough priority on your list. You get one body in this life; take care of it. Exercise will make you a better friend, girlfriend, and employee. An exercise routine will do wonders for your self-esteem because you'll feel proud of your accomplishments and friends will start to notice. If you are not currently exercising, I suggest finding accountability—either in a friend or a goal you are working toward—because it's going to be hard. Exercise not only boosts your confidence and helps you maintain a healthy weight, but it's also a great stress releaser and gives you endorphins.

Getting into healthy physical shape (not model thin—most men don't like that anyway) not only allows you to feel healthier and have more energy for things you enjoy, like time with your friends, working, or taking trips, but it also creates confidence. That confidence shines in every aspect of your life, from work to relationships.

- **Shopping.** Ruthie tells me that new clothes can make all the difference. So I want to encourage you to treat yourself to a shopping trip every once in a while. It doesn't have to be a $200 spend, just something new to make you feel beautiful and confident. If you are going on a date, buy a new outfit for the occasion. Lastly, buying a new workout outfit is great inspiration to get started at the gym. Spend money making yourself feel beautiful. You deserve it.

- **Time.** Again, the way you spend your time shows how well you care for yourself. Once a month, spend time that is all about you (sleeping and showering don't count). For Ruthie, it is sitting in a coffee shop all morning with no agenda. She loves to paint, so once a year I make her spend an afternoon painting. Other ideas for spending time just on you are signing up for a half marathon if you've always wanted to run, or joining a book club if you really love reading, or starting a garden if you have a green thumb. The only rule is you have the freedom to fail at any and all of these—because it's just about you, not accomplishing a goal.

As Albert Einstein is often quoted as saying, "The definition of insanity is doing the same thing over and over and expecting different results." Start making changes in your life to care for and respect yourself. It can make all the difference.

I Thought This Was a Dating Book?

There is a man out there right now who will one day look at you and be floored by your beauty. You were created unique—with a unique body, facial features, and skin coloring—for a reason and a purpose. As Ruthie has told you, she feels disdain for her legs on occasion. Well, the thing is those legs are one of my favorite parts about my wife. She has asked me approximately 708 times to confirm this, and I don't mind telling her each time. I've heard other stories of women who hate their hair, or skin, or figure, but their husbands adore those scorned parts. Let me assure you that you have what it takes to attract Mr. Right. Not because you are going to change your personality or inject your brow line with Botox, but because you are uniquely you: beautiful like no other.

Will you take steps today to throw off the lies that you aren't thin enough, pretty enough, funny enough, quiet enough, stylish enough—and begin to love yourself? Will you stop mentally beating up your body and start speaking some nice words to yourself?

It's time to start embracing the amazing, beautiful you. No more excuses, all right?

Real Men and the Real You
In 140 Characters or Less

#RealMenDontText

You have what it takes to attract a good man. Yes, YOU.
#RealMenDontText

Confidence is the quiet assurance you are enough.
#RealMenDontText

If you can't learn to care for & love yourself, how can you expect a man to do so?
#RealMenDontText

List qualities you love about yourself. You'll need a reminder when the world says you aren't enough.
#RealMenDontText

There is a man out there right now who will one day look at you & be floored by your beauty.
#RealMenDontText

It's time to start embracing the amazing, beautiful you. No more excuses, all right?
#RealMenDontText

CHAPTER 7

Real Red Flags

run, baby, run

REMEMBER HOW I DIDN'T WANT to be a Christian because I had all these crazy impressions of people who loved Jesus? Well, the "You might be called to singleness" mantra didn't help. If you've ever been near a church, you've probably heard at least one older single woman speak on (*gasp!*) singleness. In my case, the speaker not only was what I considered old, but also seemed to adhere to the "Christian modesty pledge," which also terrified me. After hearing her talk about being called to singleness and how she actually did enjoy her life, I fell headfirst into dating a "nice" drug dealer. I was paranoid about ending up like her and wasn't planning on waiting around to see if God "called" or didn't. As my sister once said, "If God calls me to singleness, I'm not answering."

Most of us have been there. We're single, we're strong, and we aren't settling. And then maybe it's a comment at a holiday party or our friends' lack of standards or a ticking clock—but something jolts us out of waiting for the right man and taking our relationships seriously.

As women, it's easy to start dating or "hanging out" with *that guy*, justifying the entire scenario. We tell ourselves it's just one date and we're allowed to have a little fun. Or maybe that he deserves a chance and we shouldn't be judgmental. It's just casual, and everyone should calm down, right? I've met up with guys late at night, telling myself the whole way that we weren't going to kiss. . . . You can imagine how that scenario always ended. All these relationships are casual at first—and then comfortable—and suddenly we've wasted months, if not years.

We could avoid unnecessary heartache if we simply notice the red flags in the beginning and don't continue to walk down a slippery relationship path with a man we know isn't right. I learned the hard way that most bad relationships can be avoided if we simply walk away the moment we see the warning signs. The truth is it never really is just one more date or one more night. We are always on a path either walking toward Mr. Right . . . or away from him.

In high school and college, it's easy to make excuses for our relationships because marriage seems a distant future. Our peers often encourage our irresponsible decisions, not considering how nights, months, and years of dating the wrong man are instilling in us the idea that we do not deserve a good one!

Michael and I are writing this book because we care about you and your future—because who you date at sixteen, and at twenty-two, and during that year when you are really lonely, and at forty-three *matters*. That guy you dated just to feel better about yourself? That casual college fling? They matter too. Every relationship shapes future relationships down the road. We've already talked about the consequences of sex in chapters 3 and 4, but even if you're not having sex, your current relationship will shape your expectations for what is and isn't okay in the next. If you are compromising now, it will be easier to compromise later when it really matters (i.e., when deciding who will father your children). Please don't base the second most important decision of your life on excuses.

It's Not Casual

I cannot promise you that your Jim Halpert will show up at your cubicle and sweep you off your feet or that Johnny will appear to make sure Baby doesn't get put in a corner. But I can almost guarantee that if you start dating or "hanging out" with the wrong guy to make yourself feel better or just to fill time, *you are more likely to miss the right guy.* Men will tell you how much of a turnoff it is for them to see an attractive girl with a lot of potential for a relationship hanging out with Mr. Wrong. It makes them believe there are no good girls left (Michael actually experienced this sentiment for many years).

I know he's charming. I know you have a song. I know you've never felt like this with anyone before. Maybe he is the right man for you, and your family and friends are clueless. *Maybe.* I'll let you decide, but chances are if you are explaining away the behavior of the guy you're with and consistently making excuses for him, he isn't right for you. Dating the wrong guy makes you more likely to marry the wrong guy.

It wasn't until college that I learned that every dating decision and short-term fling was shaping my future, whether I meant it to or not. It can be excruciating to hear the truth, especially when it means breaking up with Mr. Blue Eyes. I was nearly devastated when I embraced the importance of my dating decisions. I threw a couple of notebooks and cried until my eyes were red. It's hard to pry your fingers off what feels good right now for a better future. So I'm giving you permission to throw our book across the room if you need to. I'll still be here in the morning when you're ready to dig it out from behind the couch and keep learning how you deserve more.

You Are(n't) the Exception

I've come a long way from "hanging out" with Mark, the bartender from the seafood restaurant I worked at after high school. Or dating the drug dealer you'll hear more about in chapter 11. But the only reason I'm not still leaping from one bad relationship to the next—or in a terrible marriage—is because I set standards for myself, even before I believed I deserved better. I made a commitment to stop sliding into bad relationships no matter how worthless I felt or how lonely I was and no matter how much it felt like the right man would never arrive. I made tough dating calls, not because it wasn't hard to be alone, but because I discovered that no relationship is ever casual.

My hope in this chapter is to give you a list of red flags that might help you avoid one more date with the wrong guy or another disappointing relationship. I wish I'd had this list when I was dating. Because the Danger Ahead sign is often there right at the beginning; you just need to know what to look for.

This list is based on research and experience. Before you read it, I want you to understand that you are not the exception. Did I read your mind? I used to think I was the exception to every dating rule. Everyone is going to be able to conjure up a story of a friend's cousin's sister who dated someone who miraculously changed into Prince Charming—but let's base our relational decisions on being the norm, not the exception, okay? It was hard thinking I was the exception to the rule only to discover I was always wrong.

The following list of red flags isn't meant to be exhaustive, but is an attempt to help you know what to watch out for and when it's time to run. In general, these red flags will show up within the first month, if not on the first few dates—plenty of time for you to surgically remove him from your life! You know where the path leads; you just need to find the courage not to take another "casual" step in the wrong direction.

Red Flags

- **He doesn't make you feel special.** You deserve to be treated well. Don't stay with a man who makes you feel you have to earn his affection or compete with other women.

- **He doesn't ask you questions about yourself.** This is a sign of selfishness. I know a woman who finally broke because her husband of twenty years rarely asked her, "How was your day?" upon returning home from work.

- **He's narcissistic.** When everything is always about him—what he wants, when he wants it—he's a narcissist. (I know a thing or two about these types.) He has chosen you because he thinks you're the type of girl who will let him get his way.

- **He's insensitive and lacks empathy for others.** If he doesn't understand why you're upset that your coworker is in the hospital or your mom lost her job, then he's not going to be empathetic toward you, either. What will happen down the road when times are hard and you need someone to walk with you through the darkness?

- **He's critical of others.** Does he criticize the server? Is he consistently name-calling and talking about how terrible this person or that person is? If this is his pattern, it's only a matter of time before he starts with you.

- **He's overly nostalgic about the past (read: college football, his fraternity, his cars).** If you had to name the most important thing in his life, and a football team or his fraternity comes to mind, you're dealing with a guy with some whacked-out priorities.

- **He's extremely possessive.** If he asks questions about every man you interact with and accuses you of

The Man You're Dating
MR. INCONSISTENT

Elle and Dan live across town from each other and have been going on dates for five months. Their mutual love for hiking and foreign cuisine has brought them together—and Dan does everything right . . . at least when they are together. He opens doors, takes her to nice restaurants, and makes plans in advance. However, it is becoming all too consistent that Dan is inconsistent. He will take Elle on a date, and then she won't hear from him except through text for two or three weeks. But he sends her several messages a day, she explains to her wide-eyed girlfriends, who all tell Elle to play it cool and not to ask for too much. He has a demanding job and is working his way up the corporate ladder, he explains, but he really does like her and promises it won't always be this way. The problem is their dates are becoming less and less frequent, and even after asking him to be more consistent, Elle feels like she is always waiting around to see if he'll make plans. What should she do? Should Elle "play it cool" and carry out their relationship over text message until Dan gets less busy?

Unfortunately, if you live in the same city as the man you are dating and you have not seen him in several weeks, then it is time to cut ties and move on. It doesn't matter if he's the president of the United States. If he does not like you enough to figure out a way to see you—everyone has to eat, after all—then you are wasting time on someone who is frankly not that into you.

Men hate to be alone just as much as women do, so they will casually date you in order to not face night after night of loneliness. Dan probably does like Elle, but not enough to want to see her often. You deserve better—now act like it! Wait for a man who hates going even one day without seeing you.

flirting, you might have a stage-five clinger on your hands, or worse, be headed for an emotionally abusive relationship (we'll talk more about that in chapter 9). No one needs to keep tabs on you all the time. You want a relationship built on trust, not paranoia.

- **His sense of humor is off.** He jokes about inappropriate things (i.e., one-night stands, threesomes, physical violence, or anything that feels off base). His humor is giving you a glimpse into who he really is and will be in the future.

- **He overindulges in drugs or alcohol.** You might think it's funny in college that he's always drunk or takes things to the next level, but in the real world it's not funny to be irresponsible or have an addiction. Tell him to go to AA, and move on.

- **He tells his mom everything (or still lives at home).** It's time for him to break up with Mommy. No man out of high school needs to have a heart-to-heart with his mother every day.

- **He doesn't have a grown-up job and isn't actively looking for one.** Michael will address this more fully in chapter 10, but if a man can't keep a job, he won't be able to be responsible in other important areas of life either.

- **He's financially irresponsible.** If he is in a lot of debt or tries to "borrow" money from you, beware. He needs a good financial adviser, maybe a long chat with Dave Ramsey, but not a girlfriend.

- **He recently "changed" but always references his**

"**crazy past.**" Anyone who has experienced radical change will tell you it doesn't happen overnight. Make sure your guy has a long track record of staying away from whatever habits he's kicked from his old life before you start planning your wedding.

- **He just ended a relationship.** Hint: you're the rebound girl. Enough said.

- **Your family and friends think he's all wrong for you.** The people closest to you are usually worth hearing out. A man you have to constantly make excuses for (especially "He's different when it's just us") is one to stay away from.

- **He is rude to his mother.** The way a man treats his mother shows exactly how he will eventually treat you.

- **He says things like "I'm never getting married" or "I'm not good boyfriend material."** He is telling you the truth. Don't walk—run! You aren't going to change him.

- **He lies to you.** Telling lies is unacceptable. Good relationships are built on mutual trust. Chances are he's hiding more from you than you realize.

- **He asks for a video game for Christmas. Every year.** Once he grows up, you may consider dating him. Until then? Let him play his video games, and remove him from your life.

- **He doesn't read.** It doesn't have to be a book, but an educational magazine, the newspaper, something—because he needs something intelligent to talk about with his brilliant girlfriend. Amen?!

- **He has an unhealthy amount of baggage.** Of course everyone has a past, but if your boyfriend's baggage is affecting his ability to put others before himself, empathize with your struggles, and live a normal life—it's time to reevaluate. Is he dragging you down? Relationships are supposed to build us up; you are not a bad person for walking away. You will actually do him a favor by letting him go and work on his past— instead of leaning on you as a crutch. You are not a savior. You cannot rescue him.

- **He has a pornography addiction and isn't actively fighting it.** (Even worse: he doesn't see it as a problem.) Studies have shown that pornography is harmful to relationships—no matter how culture tries to say it's a harmless pastime.[1] Any kind of strange sexual behavior is a flashing red light. I have heard horror stories of women not telling their friends about strange sexual tendencies in the man they're dating and it devastating them in the long run. Marital intimacy needs to be based on trust, not fear or intimidation.

- **You are a Christian and he isn't.** If your faith is important to you, important enough that you can't imagine your kids not believing or understanding your faith, then don't date someone, even casually, who doesn't share the same faith you do. If your husband can't understand the most important part of you, think of how this will affect your intimacy,

---

1. See, for example, this study in *Psychology Today*: http://www.psychologytoday.com/blog /inside-porn-addiction/201112/is-porn-really-destroying-500000-marriages-annually.

your ability to communicate, and your day-to-day life. As Christian women, we want our husband to have a moral compass and Someone higher who holds him accountable. Those of us who are Christians aren't supposed to marry someone who doesn't know Jesus—not for punishment, but in order to avoid spending marriage pulling in opposite directions.

Now that you know all the signs of future trouble, I hope you'll find no excuses to stay in or jump into a bad relationship. Put down the phone, move out of his house, break up, get help—do whatever you need to do to put yourself on the path to finding a great relationship. You deserve the best!

Let's Talk about Sexting

When I asked my blog readers for stories about texting gone wrong, Grace's account was just one of many I received about sexting wrecking people's lives and reputations. Grace started dating a soon-to-be doctor at her Bible college, and their relationship commenced with promises for purity and putting God first. But quickly social media crept in and started muddling their great face-to-face interaction. Listen to what she said:

> I think our demise was not [the] fault of, but largely made possible by, social media. Purity became a gray area amidst steamy text messages and sexually suggestive pictures sent back and forth. I learned the power at my fingertips and did not always choose to use it for good. I distinctly remember a night where he was saying no,

and I texted him a clothed, but inviting, picture in response. . . . Minutes later, he was at my door. It's hard to imagine anyone being that power drunk, but I most certainly was. My allure extended to realms I had never known, and I simply couldn't resist.

Our relationship met its end. Not surprisingly, social media also made breaking up much more difficult. Instead of having a natural time and space to heal, suddenly a month of healthy distance was interrupted by a text that would inevitably lead to more. It felt like I couldn't break free of him or our past, so long as we could Facebook, text, or have quick access to each other at any moment.

I have since healed from heartbreak and learned more about who I was in that relationship. I've dealt with many of the heart issues that were really going on at the root of it all. But I have learned about the power of social media and have a newfound respect for it. I have let it be the thief in my relationships . . . a thief of purity, of reality, of tangible experiences, and of genuine communication.

After reading Grace's message and the other e-mails I received, I noticed the topic popping up everywhere— on morning radio shows, in conversations, and even on MTV. Anna's story is another about how sexting is killing relationships.

Anna's long-distance relationship started out as a casual conversation with a good friend. Friendship quickly turned into romance. James lived three hours away, and texting became almost their sole form of communication. Anna would feel frustrated, knowing they could have covered the same ground in thirty minutes of phone time that they did with an entire day of texting.

James finally moved home, and she felt relieved, thinking the incessant texting would cease. But while the texting slowed down, the sexting started. James told Anna that sexting was just a harmless way to relieve sexual tension that they couldn't act on because they were waiting for marriage. Instead, the sexting escalated and fueled the physical relationship they were trying to avoid. Anna knew she should stop, but she couldn't. Finally, they slept together, only to have James declare, "It just isn't working anymore." They haven't spoken in the three years since Anna sent him a final angry text. It took her as long to rebuild her confidence in herself and to start dating again.

We know real men don't text, but real men and women *certainly* don't sext. Sexting, to be clear, is the act of sending sexually explicit messages or photographs, primarily between mobile phones. According to a study conducted by the National Campaign, 20 percent of teens ages thirteen to nineteen and 33 percent of young adults ages twenty to twenty-six have sent a nude or semi-nude photograph of themselves. Additionally, 39 percent of teens and 59 percent of young adults have sent a sexually suggestive message. These statistics floored me.

Hear me—sexting is a *major* red flag. It is objectification. I cannot tell you how many women have written and told me that their "trustworthy" boyfriend sent their picture to a few friends—or to his entire phone book—after a breakup. When I was in college, a sex tape meant for a girl's boyfriend made its way around the entire campus. A sorority girl who thought it would be funny to flash the camera crew on bid day still can't outrun her naked breasts that are easily searchable online. I watched a story on MTV about a high school girl whose ex-boyfriend told her he'd get back together with her if she sent him a naked picture. She loved him, and he promised to never show or send the picture to anyone else, so she hit send. A few months later, she refused to have sex with him, and he retaliated by sending the picture to the entire school. The entire school. What seemed like an innocent, flirtatious text turned into years of therapy and lifelong scars from being called degrading names by her classmates.

Run, Baby, Run

Sending a guy a naked picture is basically saying, "Here's my body. Do whatever you want with it." You are more than a body, more than a sex object, and worth more than a guy who will use you.

It absolutely crushes my spirit to think about you sending him pictures of your naked body, not just because those pictures often end up in the wrong hands or because you can never "take it back" once it's in cyberspace, but more so because it means you have bought into our culture's idea that you need to make yourself a sex object in order to find love. You were given a beautiful body, and it was never intended to be pixelated and sent to an irresponsible little boy. He could drop you tomorrow, or next month, or next year . . . and send your body to whoever he wants. If you are in this situation, get out.

Every story my readers submitted about sexting had the same ending: no relationship. Sexting is not making you closer, it's not helping him realize you are irresistible, and it's not casual. You are too smart and beautiful and worthy of love to go down or continue down this path.

Wherever you are, it's not too late to change course. It may seem impossible to end a relationship characterized by red flags, or unrealistic to not accept another date with a guy you know is trouble, but I want you to take a broad view of your life and consider which will be harder in the long run: the heartache of walking away from a bad relationship now or the future pain if you don't? You can save yourself a lot of grief if you stop hanging out with "that guy" before it gets serious. Remember, nothing is ever casual when it comes to Mr. Wrong. It's time. Run, baby, run.

Real Red Flags
In 140 Characters or Less

#RealMenDontText

Dating the wrong guy makes you more likely
to marry the wrong guy.
#RealMenDontText

You are not the exception. Watch for the red flags,
and run if necessary.
#RealMenDontText

Your family & friends think he's all wrong for you.
#redflags #RealMenDontText

If he says, "I'm never getting married" or "I'm not good
boyfriend material"—he's telling the truth!
#redflags #RealMenDontText

Real men don't text, and certainly don't sext.
#redflags #RealMenDontText

CHAPTER 8

Real Turnoffs

how not to attract the right man

"SHE'S GOING TO HAVE a hard time getting married," I told Ruthie.

"What do you mean? Why?" Ruthie asked, surprised.

"She's attractive. But that attitude is going to scare men away." I went on to explain that it didn't matter how attractive Ruthie's friend is—a disrespectful, woe-is-me-I'm-doomed-to-remain-single attitude is going to repel most, if not all, men.

Women, many times you focus on one aspect of attracting a man—appearance, for example—and neglect other areas. I promise you that most guys are not one dimensional, like most movies and magazines (and often your friends) make us out to be. Good men do exist, and they are looking for an attractive, confident woman with deep character and a kind heart. And honestly, most of the time the reason he didn't call you after your first date had nothing to do with your appearance—but might possibly have had everything to do with something you said or did that could have been easily avoided. If only you knew!

Now for my disclaimer: it is very possible that you are doing everything right, because after all, dating isn't a formula. It can be exhausting to check off lists and follow all the "rules" and yet remain single year after year. I know because I've been there.

I've been thinking about marriage since I was in the fourth grade. By the age of seventeen, I was still not married and Y2K was approaching. The world was possibly coming to an end, and I was still *single*. The world did not end, but I also still wasn't married. Then college—doesn't everyone meet their soul mate in college? Well, I didn't, despite prayer and searching. I saw my friends marry off one by one afterward, and there were times of strength and definitely moments of loneliness and weakness. Had God forgotten me?

I moved to Germany for the remainder of my twenties. Those five years overseas were not exactly the way I would have written them, but I can honestly say I would not forfeit a minute of my time there, because they were rich with experiences, albeit lonely. I want to assure you that your single status does not mean you are doing something wrong. I would never want to add an ounce of pain or shame to an already weary soul.

But in order to shoot straight with you and help you successfully navigate your dating life, I've compiled a list of mistakes—turnoffs—to most guys that are looking for a long-term relationship. Some of you may be making these easily fixable mistakes, so ask a trusted friend to tell you the truth.

Reasons Why You Might Still Be Single

- **You're a complainer.** If your life is always "just so hard" or every other day is "*the* worst day ever!" you are probably a complainer. Guys like girls who aren't always the victim. Everyone has bad days, struggles, and hardships, but try to take your pain in stride and learn from it.

- **You're disrespectful.** Or worse, you put him down in public. Even if he doesn't pick up on your disrespect because he is infatuated with you, trust me, his friends will, and they will tell him. Showing a man respect will speak volumes in a world where every other show and commercial makes fun of the dumb, good-for-nothing man. If you're an eye roller, check your attitude at the door.

- **You're desperate.** You have that look in your eye. Guys can spot the girls who are just looking for a ring a mile away. Don't ask leading questions, don't interview him, and don't tell him about your biological clock. We men are onto you. We know *exactly* what you're after.

- **You're too independent.** Is "I don't need a man" plastered on your forehead? Let your guard down a little. Chances are you have been hurt in the past. Seek some counseling and take small steps back into the dating game. If you are constantly complaining about the "lack of good men," your bitterness will come out on your dates. Every guy I know likes to be helpful and needed by a woman every now and then, even if she seems to have it all together. Let him help you sometimes, because the truth is we need each other. If you are too self-sufficient, it might scare men away.

- **You're impolite.** Do you get exasperated with your server if he or she "just can't get it right"? Do you make sure the server knows you are annoyed? Trust me, it makes a guy feel uncomfortable. He isn't going to ask you out again, because he knows that attitude will eventually attack him. Kindness is important.

- **You're a snob.** Do you pry about how much he makes? Do you brag or complain to your friends about his income? You don't want to make him wonder if he can afford you. No Mr. Right wants to be loved for his money *or* wants to feel like less of a man because he can't afford your expensive tastes.

- **You're an oversharer.** If after two or three dates he already knows all the dating mistakes you have made and all your family drama, and you've already cried on his shoulder—yep, you guessed it, you're an oversharer. Part of the beauty of pursuing a woman is the mystery. Let him in over time.

- **You talk about yourself too much.** Are you the center of attention everywhere you go? Do you thrive on that? There needs to be room for him in the conversation too.

- **You don't take care of yourself.** I'm not saying you

have to work out every day, but men can tell if you take care of yourself and eat healthy. It doesn't matter what size you wear—just take care of the body God gave you.

- **You're appearance obsessed.** Do you have to run six miles every day or count calories obsessively? Does it take you an hour to get ready to go to the grocery store? Men really appreciate a woman who looks nice and takes care of herself, but they want more than just a body. Strive for a well-balanced lifestyle.

- **Everything is a big joke to you.** You hide your feelings behind humor, inside jokes, or in ironic timings. Guys want someone to connect with emotionally, so let down your guard little by little.

- **It just may not be your time yet.** Just because you are

text translation 101

PROFESSOR: MICHAEL DEAN

Her: Hey! I'm out with the girls. Will I see you tonight?

Him: Potentially.

Her: I hope so! Do you want to meet up later?

Him: Sure. Let me talk to the boys, but it might work.

Situation: You really like this guy, but you haven't heard from him in a few weeks. Tired of waiting for him to contact you, you shoot him a harmless text.

Translation: It's doubtful the man on the other end of your text is Mr. Right. If you have to pester him to see you, he's not that interested.

Response: Turn your phone off and start preparing yourself for Mr. Right. Guys don't value easy—if he likes you, he doesn't need a text to remind him of his feelings.

single it doesn't mean you are doing something wrong. Keep up the good work and keep waiting for Mr. Right. Contrary to popular opinion, he does exist!

Turn-Ons for Mr. Right

Enough with the "wrongdoing"—let's talk about what you can do to attract Mr. Right. Here are a few turn-ons.

- **Direction.** It is important to have direction—knowing what you want in a family, in life, in a husband, and not just aimlessly hopping from job to job waiting for a man to walk into the local coffee shop where you journal about your love life to sweep you off your feet. When I met Ruthie, I loved that she had separate dreams and didn't just jump on the Michael Dean bandwagon. Are you a career woman? A more stay-at-home-mom type? Do you want five kids? Whatever your answer is—don't apologize or hide who you are! Embrace it.

- **Standards.** Men respect standards in a woman. "I won't have sex with you until we are married"; "I don't do sleepovers"; "You have to call me if you want to ask me out on a date"; "Let's do something besides watch a movie." Standards will keep the right men calling back and the wrong ones running for the hills. Exactly what you want.

- **Confidence.** Be confident in who you are, and don't try to be someone else. There will be a man out there who will love you for your quirky habits. Don't try to be the "funny one," the "flirty one," or the "hipster one" if you aren't. Ruthie loves to tell stories (with a little exaggeration), and it's hilarious! She doesn't try to be anyone else but herself. I love to see her true self come out.

- **Poise and manners.** Be a lady. Men don't want another spitting, scratching, cussing guy around—they want a lady. Ladies can hunt, hike, wear Chacos, and not wear makeup; but don't become one of the guys just to get his attention. And please avoid saying things like "I gotta pee." I cringe writing it because it's gross. There have got to be classier ways to excuse yourself to the bathroom. Be polite to his mother and his coworkers, and learn proper table manners. You don't have to wear heels every day, but make sure that the mystery of what makes you a lady stays intact. It is super attractive!

- **Family oriented.** Most men are looking for a woman who values her family. Every family comes with its share of struggles, but a commitment to family and to starting a family is an attractive trait. One of the things that I told Ruthie when I proposed was that I wanted her to be the mother of my children.

- **Passionate about others.** Guys are attracted to women who are considerate and caring toward others. If the only thing on your mind is the latest *People* magazine or how all your friends have more designer jeans than you do, the right guy might be turned off. Ruthie is passionate about other women—your hearts, your minds, and helping you respect your bodies. She has drive and cares deeply for others. This passion is incredibly attractive to me because it means that she has something else on her mind besides herself.

Mr. Right is looking for a woman who is more than just a pretty face; he is looking for a woman with deep character, one who challenges him to be better and stronger. Each of you can be the right woman the right man is looking for—it just may take time for him to notice your stunning, confident, grace-filled self.

Real Turnoffs
In 140 Characters or Less

#RealMenDontText

Good men do exist, and they are looking for a confident woman with deep character and a kind heart.
#you #RealMenDontText

Reason #2 you are single: You're disrespectful.
realturnoffs #RealMenDontText

Reason #4 you are single: You're too independent. You have "I don't need a man" plastered on your forehead.
#realturnoffs #RealMenDontText

Find life direction. Want something more in life than just a husband.
#realturn-ons #RealMenDontText

Men are attracted to women who are passionate about other people. Be caring and considerate.
#realturn-ons #RealMenDontText

CHAPTER 9

Real Women Stop Making Excuses

he's not your last chance

"HE'S MY LAST CHANCE," she said.

My friend Jen tends to ramble, so I have to admit I was only half listening to her stories about Zumba classes, her lunatic landlord, and whatever else was on her mind. But that comment snapped my thoughts back to our conversation.

"Your last chance? You don't really believe that . . ." I trailed off, noting it wasn't just an offhanded comment. She truly believed her boyfriend, Matt, was her "last chance" at love.

Jen, like many other women I counsel, believed she was at a crossroads where one direction led to mediocre marriage and the other yielded a life of always driving herself to the airport and sleeping in the middle of the bed. It seemed obvious to her that a life with Mr. Not-So-Perfect was far more desirable than a life alone.

A server came and took our order—salmon for me, steak for her—poured more wine, and refilled the crumb-dusted bread basket. Two breadbaskets, wine, and an early request for the dessert menu was our way of coping with this post-modern dating world.

I had just ended a long-term relationship with a great guy, someone I knew wasn't right for me—so I was just as unsure of my future as Jen. The week before, I had tried to get back together with that ex-boyfriend after an older single mentor insisted great guys are hard to find and I needed to hang on to one while I was young.

Jen was my friend who always had someone. The girl with all the right proportions, enhanced by a flirty nature that made her a magnet in bars. She had a wandering spirit about her, so she'd tried every career from marketing to selling jewelry to life coaching. This month she was teaching Zumba classes.

"He's not that bad. Just sometimes unpredictable and a tad aggressive with his words. And plus, we have tons of chemistry," she said, soaking her bread in olive oil.

We talked about the lack of good men and whether or not she should settle for someone "good enough" or wait and risk not finding someone extraordinary. Our entrées came on plates speckled with fresh ground pepper, and we ordered chocolate lava cake for dessert. Jen and Matt had dated on and off for three years, and she felt it would be senseless to start all over. She reminded me of our friends' rough dating stories. I listened, feeling that she should walk away, but not entirely convinced. After all, they had already been through so much together—Matt's father passing the year before and Jen's many career changes.

"I'm just going to see how things go," she finally concluded. It sounded like a great middle-of-the-road response—but the truth is we are always on a path either to better relational decisions or worse ones. Every road leads somewhere.

Three years passed and Jen and Matt got engaged, but he broke off the engagement three months before the wedding, telling her, "This was *never* what I wanted." Her heart shattered.

I wonder how Jen's life—and mine and yours—would have been different if we had stopped making excuses sooner? What would it be like to stop pretending you aren't on a path to a life with the wrong guy?

The Excuses We Make

I know the man you're dating . . . because I've dated him too. He's the guy you are constantly making excuses for. Sometimes the excuses are to your friends, sometimes just to yourself. "He's different when we're alone together." "He had a hard childhood." "He's looking for a job—it's not like I have to marry Bill Gates, right?" "He's changing!"

You don't say? I dated a fixer-upper too. Whenever you are converting oxygen into carbon dioxide, you are listing reasons why it's okay to stay together. You know something isn't quite right, but you keep excusing away his behavior—his tardiness, his faithlessness, his deadbeatness—whatever makes him all wrong for you. You saw red flags in the beginning—ignored them—and now you feel like you're too far into the relationship to make a U-turn.

"It won't happen to me" is exactly what everyone thinks about bad relationships. Because no one ever wakes up and says, "I think I'll drive my life off a cliff by getting into a bad relationship" or "I'll have kids with a man who will be a terrible father." You probably look at divorced couples and think it will never be you—you would never make the mistake of marrying the wrong guy. But divorced women are just like you and me—women wanting to be loved and often unsure of what love looks like.

In high school, I went to a party, and the guys standing outside made us spin around to make sure we "qualified" to come in. Was being "hot" enough to get into a party what it felt like to be loved? Was the guy who showered me with attention all night and asked me to sit on his lap loving me? Was it love when he told me I was the hottest girl he'd ever seen and asked me to go into the bedroom with him? Of course not—but how was I to know better? I didn't know what a good relationship looked like or felt like or what to watch out for. I looked for love in all the wrong places. If you're in a bad relationship characterized by excuses, it's going to be a hard road to end it. But better now than later.

This kind of love is like walking into the ocean on a clear blue day. Your senses are intoxicated with the smell of the salt and the gentle breeze. The placid waters seem like they will only ever flow tenderly against your body. But when a tidal wave comes, it can be so violent and scary that most people just stand still. Most women spend years trying to become better swimmers in the torrent instead of doing everything they can to get back to shore. I challenge you to take the red flags seriously and not try to brave the winds when you see signs of a storm brewing. It's time to get out.

I want to look at several excuses I've used that might help you determine whether or not you are wasting your time with the wrong man.

- **"He's changing."** I put this excuse first for a very important reason. He's most likely not changing—and you're not helping him by making excuses. I cannot tell you how many men I tried to "change." In high school, my efforts were focused on Phillip. He wasn't a Christian, and I wanted to change him into one. Didn't happen. Freshman year of college, Robbie had an ego problem and a drinking problem. I believed my love would help him stop drinking and humble him. It didn't. The next year, I made a commitment to only date someone if he checked the "Christian" box—so I began a relationship with Brandon just hours after he became a Christian. He had a drinking problem and some violent tendencies. I didn't change him, either.

  I know he makes promises, but your making excuses for his anger or laziness or lack of direction actually only fuels his ability to stay right where he is. And marriage will not change him; in fact, marriage usually makes issues worse. If your relationship is based on the fact that your guy "will change" or "is changing," I challenge you to step away and see if he's serious about making the necessary alterations to his life.

- **"We've already slept together."** Especially if you've grown up in the church, losing your virginity to someone can make you feel like a failure and heap on the shame. Someone very close to me slept with a guy in college and continued to date him because she thought she could "make up for" her sin by marrying the guy. She didn't want to have a string of sexual partners behind her when she met the right man, so she married the first man she slept with, out of guilt more than love. Please hear me that you are not a failure—far from it! Your past does not define you. Basing a marriage on a lapse in judgment or a guilty conscience is setting yourself up to fail.

- **"I'm basically already part of his family."** This excuse is a common reason why women stay with boyfriends longer than they should—because breaking up feels like losing a boyfriend and a family. I remember that when I broke up with my college boyfriend I was almost more devastated to lose my relationship with his parents. I'm not saying it's not hard, but you can't base a marriage on family members you'll see occasionally. No matter how much his shiny family helps his image, at the end of the day it's about the two of you. If you wouldn't consider a future with him if his family weren't in the picture, it's time for a breakup.

- **"I don't want to be alone."** You need time alone to

work on preparing yourself to be the right woman the right man is looking for. Again, filling your time with "that guy" makes you more likely to miss the right man. No one likes to be dateless, but we're talking delayed gratification for better sex, better communication, and a better marriage later.

- **"We've been together so long. I don't want to start over."** I have many friends who have been in five- and six-year relationships. Are you scared of starting over? Michael and I have only known each other for four years, so I don't know exactly what this feels like, but I do know that "waiting it out" to see if he proposes or gets his act together isn't going to do anything other than waste more time (yours and his). It's scary to start over after you've invested so much time and energy in one person—but tomorrow and next week and next month and next year it's going to be even harder.

- **"He had a hard childhood."** I'm not advocating for not being gracious with people in your life, but if he continually mentions trauma in his past to gain sympathy from you, he has a victim mentality. You can be friends with him, but your relationship with a man who treats you as a parent rather than a partner is a very bumpy road—one you don't want to take another step down.

- **"We've been through so much together."** A woman recently shared with me that she couldn't break up with her boyfriend because he had supported her through her mother's painful passing away. A friend shared she couldn't end her relationship because her boyfriend had battled cancer, and as she said, "you have no idea how close we became going through something like that." If a tragic life event or series of experiences has bonded you and your boyfriend, great! But not so great if you know you shouldn't be with him anymore—or maybe shouldn't have been with him in the first place. Someone with long-term potential won't keep you mentioning "how much" you've been through together.

- **"We're not serious."** I hate to beat this one into the ground, but every relationship is serious whether or not you label it that way. Relationships program our minds as to what is and isn't an acceptable way to be treated. I know many people who entered a casual, no-big-deal relationship with red lights flashing overhead and never did get out. Furthermore, no man deserves to be a placeholder while you wait for someone better.

- **"I'm never going to meet anyone as _____ as he is."** I've heard excuses like "But I'll never meet someone as funny as he is"; "But no one will ever get me like he does"; "No man could love me as much as he does." If you are staying with a man who isn't treating you well just because you are afraid you'll never find someone else with similar traits, it's time for a breakup. Wait for the man who is good husband

and father material and who thinks your quirky dance moves rival Michael Jackson's.

- **"It's too late to meet anyone else."** Too old? Too long gone? Too many bad relationships in your pocket? It is never too late to start learning respect and love for yourself—no matter what your past or your birth date indicates. Think about it: if you are too old or too "messed up" to meet the right man, why would you make excuses to date the wrong ones? Dating men who don't respect you will only reinforce your disrespect for yourself. It's never too late to stop making excuses.

Emotional Abuse

"I thought I was the luckiest girl in the world—until he became a monster."

Finley's boyfriend was a great man in the beginning—kind, complimentary, and considerate. Within a month, he started talking about meeting her family and confessing he wanted to marry her. She was a little alarmed but brushed her concern aside because she'd known other couples that had jumped on the fast track to marriage.

As the weeks went by, he gradually changed—so gradually and subtly that Finley couldn't really identify what she was experiencing. He would use the Bible as an excuse for his name-calling or forced kissing, because "God understands how sinful we are." He started demanding to know where she was at all times and making her change important plans to come visit him, threatening to leave her if she didn't comply.

Finley tried to break up with him over and over, but to no avail. He would always apologize with big displays of flowers and affection and promises to never act the same way again. After he called her stupid or put her in uncomfortable sexual situations, he would turn around and do wonderful things for her and her family. Finally, Finley broke it off with him for good. Now aware that what she experienced was emotional abuse, she challenges other women to examine their relationships.

"I'm scared, angry, and confused. I love God and pray often, but I am hurt and frustrated that He allows the situation to continue. I don't know what to do or where to go. I feel very broken and alone."

Lillian's relationship went sour when her boyfriend, who was sixteen years older, wouldn't let her break up with him. "If I can't have you, no one can!" he said. Lillian turned her back on all her friends to devote her time and heart to her boyfriend. He showed her attention she didn't receive at home. He whispered sweet nothings in her ear, followed by threats—of leaving, of hurting her, of exposing who she really was. Lillian started to feel worthless. She stopped thinking about leaving him, because she came to believe she didn't deserve better. Lillian married her abuser and had three sons with him.

"He would cry himself to sleep most nights over the pain from his childhood."

Janie's relationship seemed fine on the exterior, but she slowly started to feel trapped. Adam told her he'd been suicidal before they met and Janie was "healing" him. But then

The Man You're Dating
MR. FIXER-UPPER

Nicole and Sam meet at a runner's group in Nashville—which Sam began as a part of his recovery. He's started AA and for the first time in his life feels like he can actually change. At first he and Nicole are just friends; but over time, casual run-ins downtown commence, and one night everything clicks. Sam professes his love for Nicole, and they start dating. A few months later Sam relapses, spirals downward, and loses his job. Nicole's feelings for him are very strong, and she can't walk away. She vows to help him get back on his feet. After all, doesn't he need her now more than ever?

Nicole stays with Sam. He gets better and then relapses. One night he cheats on her, but she takes him back because she loves him unconditionally. Sam continues in the same pattern and still has shaky employment.

It's tempting to pick out a wounded, hurting man who needs you—but you know what? Mr. Fixer-Upper doesn't make a great partner. Nicole should have told Sam how much she cared about him . . . and walked out the door. If your guy is serious about change, let him change on his own. If he cares enough about you, he'll do it. If he isn't willing to change on his own, you won't change him, no matter how hard you try.

he started criticizing her for all sorts of faults, especially her weight. He was drunk most weekends; when she'd ask him to stop drinking, he would bring up her love of eating. It always turned into a fight, and she tried to break up several times, but "I was afraid he would break, and how could I live with myself if I caused him to go over the edge?" Toward the end of their third year together, he started grabbing her clothes and threatening her. Janie finally had the courage to leave Adam, but she says that even four years later, the relationship still deeply affects her ability to trust.

All these relationships have a common denominator: emotional abuse. If you read these stories and thought, *I'd never let this happen to me* or *He would never treat me this way*, think again. Thirty-five percent of women have been in emotionally abusive relationships, so it's more common than we realize.[1]

Emotional abuse can take on many different forms and can be difficult to recognize. One woman thought her boyfriend wanted to know where she was at all times because he loved her so much. Another figured her man was just being kind and trying to decrease the stress in her life when he asked her to quit her job and stay home. Yet another felt that her relationship was changing her personality—she didn't like to dance or enjoy time with friends anymore. Abusers are good manipulators. They tend to smooth over their bad behavior and make you believe it's your fault. Even if you can't imagine yourself ever being in an abusive situation, I

---

1. Martha Brockenbrough, "Is Your Partner Emotionally Abusive?" *Women's Health* (March 2010): http://www.womenshealthmag.com/sex-and-relationships/emotional-abuse.

still think it's important to learn the signs that the man in your life deserves nothing but the dust behind you.

Here are some characteristics of an emotionally abusive relationship:

- Makes you constantly feel nervous or like you're walking on eggshells around him. *"One of these days you'll wake up and I'll be gone."*
- Asks you to change jobs or careers, or even quit a job, because he wants you home (i.e., to control you). *"I want you to stay home so I can keep an eye on you."*
- Is extremely jealous and accuses you of flirting with other men; lashes out when you have a simple conversation. *"Why are you always disrespecting me in public and flirting with other men?"*
- Constantly needs to know where you are, who you are with, and what you are doing (i.e., even time with girlfriends is monitored as closely as if you were his child). *"You shouldn't spend so much time and money shopping for clothes; you don't have a good figure anyway."*
- Puts you down, calls you names, or criticizes you. *"You are such a _____—it's a wonder I put up with you."*
- Makes you feel like you can't do anything right or blames you for his problems. *"You don't know the first thing about finances."*
- Makes you feel like no one else would want you. *"Don't complain about how bad you have it—do you think anyone else would put up with you?"*

- Threatens to hurt you, your friends, or your family—but then says he was just "overreacting" or "kidding."
- Checks your cell phone or e-mail without permission.
- Asks you to change your lifestyle, personality, hobbies, and/or job.
- Treats you like a project—campaigns for you to lose weight, whiten your teeth, get organized, etc.
- Fights like a jerk. And then apologizes with flowers and big displays of affection.

An abuser wants you to think that you are the problem. If you find yourself walking on eggshells, constantly thinking about how to avoid upsetting him, believing it's all your fault—I encourage you to take the steps to talk to a trusted friend or counselor about abuse. You are worth loving, and I pray you know how deeply you are loved. I can't say much about my history with this subject, but I understand what you are going through. I promise it won't be easy to cut ties, but I also promise you'll never regret it.

When You Marry the Wrong Guy

In the midst of thinking through this chapter, I came up for air from writing and attended a college football game with my father-in-law. We found our seats in the packed-out stadium—and then I saw her. A twentysomething anxiously gnawing her nails and intermittently slurping what looked to be a hot chocolate. She was scanning the crowd, looking for someone. *Maybe her husband*, I thought, noting her wedding ring. *But why is she so on edge?*

As a writer, it's my job to notice people around me. I'm not an observant person by nature, but writing has taught me to look, and look closely. People's external behavior isn't what is important; it's just the arrow that points to the "why" hidden under the surface. There is always a story behind why people act the way they do; it often just takes listening to deeper cries, the aches, the longings that remain unseen.

The woman continued to gnaw on her nails and started pacing. Then she waved, and the man I later discovered was her husband came bounding up the bleachers, hot dog and Styrofoam cup in hand. And then it started.

Her husband was a profanity-screaming lunatic. My father-in-law and I were shocked, trying to sit calmly amid a sea of fans, cringing at the language coming out of this guy's mouth. He was right behind us and was spitting with every word, clearly intoxicated. *Oh no.*

He was also intermittently yelling, "My wife is hot," so I knew he was married to the anxious woman beside him. As he would try to antagonize fans who were calmly finding their seats, his wife would apologize and attempt to assuage his hostility. Everyone was standing, but she sat down.

The national anthem started, and her husband continued to spew violent, angry words. My father-in-law stepped over and put a hand on his shoulder, saying sternly, "Please be respectful."

"Watch it, old man! I will drop you. Touch me one more time . . ." The guy lurched forward, beer in hand, trying to pick a fight. The tension in the crowd around us was steadily increasing, but I kept it together until the next scene.

His wife begged him to calm down and not get in a fight. She put her delicate hand with a shiny diamond over his mouth and pleaded, "Don't do this, please."

"You need to sitdowwwwn and shut up." And then again, louder and more vicious. He hurled insult after insult at his wife—horrible, demeaning words. For a moment, I wanted to cry for her. I could not imagine Michael speaking to me in such a violent manner. But then my sadness dissipated, and I was filled with anger. I jumped across my father-in-law, got right in the guy's face, pointed my finger, and yelled at him.

I'm not really sure what all I said, but I know I told him what a gift his wife is and how he has no right to treat her like trash.

My father-in-law stopped me after he thoroughly enjoyed seeing me wave my finger and let this guy have it for a few seconds. Another fan went and got the police, who promptly corralled the guy.

I could have ignored the profanity and the screaming at the Vanderbilt players and fans—but not at his wife. I could not stand by and listen to him speak to someone he had pledged his life to like she was a trashed stadium cup. The thought of how he must treat her at home made me want to reach out and hug this girl who now stared blankly down onto the field. I knew she wasn't watching the game.

Why would she marry him?

Why does any man or woman get into a bad relationship? I wondered when the first signs of his anger problems surfaced and what went through her head. I considered how many sleepless nights she must have faced before walking down the aisle, unsettled about his outbursts, verbal abuse, and anger. I wondered how many different promises he'd made to change.

Maybe she believed he would change when they got married. Maybe she didn't know she deserved better, because another man in her life told her she was worthless too. Did she have a bad relationship with her father?

I'll never know.

But what I do believe is that as the storm grew fiercer and fiercer, the waves higher, she just tried to swim faster. Her love for him overwhelmed any sense of danger. He didn't suddenly morph into a screaming, abusive lunatic. She made excuses. Maybe just a few, maybe a hundred—but she excused away his behavior.

I'll never forget that game. I was awakened yet again to exactly how serious our dating decisions are—and I beg you to consider the red flags, the question marks, the subtle ways you try to sweep concerns away. If you've ignored all the red flags and are in a rocky relationship, it's important to walk away before you make a permanent commitment. The scary part about love is I don't believe we can always help who we fall in love with. But I do believe that swimming back to safety, away from the storm, is always a choice, no matter how much you love someone.

Marriage doesn't change, fix, or heal people—whatever red flag you see in your significant other will only be magnified in marriage. Maybe it's not verbal abuse, but a character deficit in other areas. Maybe he doesn't want your kids raised in church and you do. May you have the courage to stop making excuses and walk away—for both yourself and future generations. Don't settle for crumbs when you were made for more. So much more.

Real Women Stop Making Excuses
In 140 Characters or Less

#RealMenDontText

He isn't your last chance at love! Time for a breakup.
#noexcuses #RealMenDontText

Common excuse to stay with Mr. Wrong #4.
"He is changing!" No he isn't!
#noexcuses #RealMenDontText

Common excuse to stay with Mr. Wrong #5.
"We already slept together."
#noexcuses #RealMenDontText

Emotional abuse can take many forms. Does he
make you feel bad for just being you?
#RealMenDontText

Marriage doesn't change, fix, or heal anyone;
whatever red flags you see will only be
more significant in marriage.
#RealMenDontText

CHAPTER 10

Real Men Grow Up

finding a man with direction

LOVE CAN'T GET YOU THROUGH . . . a direction problem. When you're young, it's easy to be attracted to the carefree waiter or the burly trainer, without a thought of what your life will look like if the two of you settle down. In love, no one wants to face the reality of what life will be in ten years, but it's important for every woman, no matter her age, to ask, "Does the man I'm dating have direction? Does he know where he's going? What will our life look like in ten or twenty years if we marry?" A man's direction is one of the most important things about him and often defines who he is. Nothing against the barista or valet—I was one—but if that is all he is aspiring to, then "love can get us through" isn't enough to make a relationship last. Eventually, the chemistry will fade, and you need to think about what will be left.

All We Need Is Love?

By definition, a man with direction knows where he's going and has the drive to get there. Then you can decide if his vision for life matches up with your vision. I'm telling you, this life path question is more important than most realize. When you're in love, it's nearly impossible to pick your head up and ask the hard questions. But ask you must, because you don't want to wind up like a friend of mine who married a man who didn't know where he was headed—then one morning he announced without warning, "I'm called to move to China for missions work." She was devastated because she hated traveling, didn't do well with foreign cultures, and enjoyed her life in the States. If going on fancy vacations to the Caribbean every winter is what you imagine for your life, great! But in that case don't marry a plumber and expect to be a stay-at-home mom with a new SUV.

A man with direction will be a good leader and a good father because he has confidence in himself. Many men feel that what they do is the most important thing about them—in the same way women often feel their relationships are the most important aspect of who they are. A man with direction feels good about going to parties and meeting new people, because he's proud of what he has accomplished. He will also be intentional with your relationship; without direction, he usually won't commit, because of insecurity.

In today's economy it can be difficult for a man to land his dream job or even start a career, but that isn't an excuse for him not to strive to reach his full potential. In this chapter I will help you understand the deeper desires of men and the challenges we are facing today. Not to enable you to lower your standards or let men off the hook—but to inform you of the difference between a guy you should run from and a guy who just needs a little encouragement in this part of his life. I was a guy who needed some encouragement. Here is part of the story of my struggle with direction.

I was "let go" . . . which we all know means I was fired. Ruthie and I were just a few months away from our wedding day, and losing my job was not part of the plan. I had taken a job in the "real world" after I moved home from Germany, where I worked in ministry. The job sounded like a great transition. The problem was that it was in a warehouse, and I was clearly not cut out for operating large machinery and taking inventory (i.e., I was a bad counter). After I crashed the forklift for the third time, it was obvious my calling was elsewhere.

It's hard for a man to admit that he's not good at something—especially something that seems to come easily to others. Failure always feels personal.

When I was in Germany, I was well thought of and an expert in my field. I was the area director and had responsibility managing people and resources. I could talk to kids about Jesus, plan weeklong service trips, coach basketball, and cast vision for the leaders I was responsible for. Translation: I felt important.

So when Ruthie and I came back from our honeymoon and she scurried off to work the next morning, I didn't quite know what to do with myself. For weeks I cleaned the house, organized our wedding presents, and worked one or two days a week as a valet. Valet parking was less than ideal for my self-esteem—running after cars doesn't exactly give you a sense of accomplishment. I started to feel worthless and beat down. Then helplessness set in as rejection e-mails hit my in-box from different jobs I'd applied for. I didn't have a clue what I wanted to do or how to go about figuring it out. Ruthie would come home from work each day exhausted; I would see my new bride walking through the door and feel horrible that I didn't have any good job news to share with her.

Then the endless mind numbing set in: YouTube. Craigslist. Netflix. Whatever I could find to take my mind off the fact that I was nearly thirty and felt like direction had eluded me. Ruthie wasn't sure what to do with my unraveling self-esteem and hours spent on the lonely Internet. It was a delicate time for our marriage.

I tell you this story so that you can figure out what kind of man you are dating with three questions: Does the man I am dating/interested in have direction? Does the man I'm dating not have a clue what comes next? Or, does the man I'm dating have direction but need some encouragement?

As men we feel defined by what we do. Right or wrong, it is a symptom of a deeper problem that all men deal with: significance. We are told that our significance is derived from our occupation, our ability to provide, make money, score a basket, or succeed at what we consider important tasks. This is why men work out, buy big trucks, try to date the "hot" girl, and become workaholics—to feel significant, to prove ourselves. We do okay until something unravels and we have to face the core of who we are. We ask the question, Do I matter?—bringing us face-to-face with where we find our significance. You want a man who is not afraid to ask the hard questions of himself. Does he believe he has greater significance than just what he can bring home? Does he know that he is created in love and has worth?

Just as women are not defined by the number of men complimenting their beauty, men are not defined by their jobs, but many of us grow up hearing messages that we don't have what it takes. These lies can cripple men, preventing them from finding the right direction—and often turning them into the man-boys Ruthie and I are trying to stop you from dating.

Many of us have never had a

text translation 101

PROFESSOR: MICHAEL DEAN

Him: Hey, I need you.

Her: Oh no, what's wrong?

Him: I'm about to break down, I really need you.

Her: Okay, on my way, is anyone there with you?

Him: No, I feel safer with you.

Her: Of course! Stay calm and breathe.

Situation: You meet a guy at a friend's house and things click. After a couple of dates you realize that he has some hard issues he is working through, and he starts coming to you to talk or for advice.

Translation: He is probably a great guy, but he doesn't need you—he needs professional help from a counselor or therapist. He's not ready for a relationship.

Response: Keep a safe distance so that he does not view you as his "rock" in these hard times. That is a hard place for a relationship to start off, and chances are if the relationship goes further, your needs are not going to be met.

father or a father figure take an interest in our development. This cultural trend means many of us have had to figure out manhood all on our own. Even in homes where fathers are present, oftentimes these fathers are relationally absent. It is tragic. I have a very close friend whose dad habitually called him demeaning names, doing serious damage to his self-worth. A man's relationship with his father has a direct impact on the way he feels about himself, and in turn the way he treats you as a woman. Most men have never been taught the proper way to provide for, love, and cherish you. So what can you do?

Helping Mr. Directionally Challenged

My job situation and unraveling self-esteem created many sleepless nights for Ruthie. She hated to see me so down on myself and wasn't quite sure how to address the issue without stepping on my pride. At first, I was on job websites every day and frantically sending out résumés, but over time, I lost hope. Every no confirmed that I wasn't good enough. My situation was every man's deepest fear.

Fortunately for me, Ruthie was gracious in that she didn't turn into a nagging mother, but she also didn't coddle and make excuses for me. I didn't need a mother, and I didn't need a babysitter—I needed a loving wife to challenge me. She would sit with me and tell me what I would be great at, slowly restoring my confidence. Ruthie helped me look for jobs, write cover letters, and edit my résumé. She believed in me when I didn't believe in myself. She also pointed me to the counsel of wiser men, men who had direction in their lives. Exactly what I needed.

Ladies, I want you to clearly understand that you are not to make excuses for your boyfriend's joblessness or lack of direction—but you can give him a shot at making things right. I understand that this is a very fine line for you to walk. But you can do it with grace for a couple of months and see if you notice real change. There is a difference between a man who is simply out of a job and one without direction.

Practical Ways to Help Him Find Direction

- Encourage him to talk to his dad, a male mentor, or a man he respects. He needs someone other than you helping him navigate this difficult season of his life.
- Tell him he has what it takes. These words show respect, and all men want to feel respected. It makes us feel valuable and loved.
- Remind him how much you believe in him. As often as you want to hear you are beautiful, he wants to hear you believe in him and respect him.
- Avoid controlling or nagging. He already has a mother and doesn't need a second.
- Don't give him an easy way out (i.e., don't write his résumé for him as he plays video games). He needs to have some investment in finding direction.
- Ask him what he's passionate about. Ask, "What would you do if you knew you couldn't fail?" Help him brainstorm about realistic careers, connections, and job opportunities.

- Be patient and speak kindly—you are dealing with the most sensitive part of a man's heart. Avoid absolute statements, and speak about his actions rather than his character. (Instead of "You are a lazy, good-for-nothing slacker," try "I feel like you aren't taking your career seriously when you don't apply for a single job all week.")
- Set your standards so he knows what you expect—you aren't easy, and you won't wait around forever for him to step up. He has two months. He should be able to find direction within that time, whether that is starting a career path, a job, or a degree.

If you follow the steps above, you might be able to steer your guy in the right direction, but keep in mind that you can't save him. Ladies, this isn't easy work, I know. Good men are out there—I know a lot of them and have seen hundreds comment on Ruthie's blog agreeing with this very content.

On the other hand, you might be dating a man with a "direction problem"—something deeper that can't be fixed no matter how much encouragement, résumé editing, and patience you dish out. Here are some indications that this might be the case:

- He leaves a job because it's "hard." His workload is terrible, his boss is difficult, his customers are always griping, his salary is unfair. . . . You get the idea.
- He is thirty-five and still waiting for his "big break."

That train left the station about ten years ago; it's time to find a career and stick with it.

- He moves from "calling" to "calling." Two years ago he was going to be an artist, last year he wanted to be a carpenter, and this year he wants to be a triathlete sponsored by Nike. These guys have deeper issues and never feel settled.
- His long-term plan includes the words "no idea" or "Starbucks has good benefits."
- He doesn't want to work and asks you if you can help him financially until he gets back on his feet. Thirty days? Fine. A few years? Disaster.
- He is waiting for that "perfect job" and is not willing to do anything in the meantime. Most job suggestions insult his intelligence.

A man with direction will pull his weight in your relationship, both now and when family and finances are big issues. You will be able to feel safe with him because he comes through for you. You want a man who will take his responsibilities seriously and not constantly need you to pick up his slack. The men of our generation are experiencing a crisis of direction, so give your guy a chance to find it and offer him help. But don't stay with a joker who is keeping you around because you put up with him. Circle the day on the calendar, and break it off if nothing changes.

Real Men Grow Up
In 140 Characters or Less

#RealMenDontText

By definition, a man with direction knows where he is going in life and has the drive to get there.
#RealMenDontText

A man with direction is a good leader and good father because he has confidence in himself.
#RealMenDontText

Men are not defined by their jobs, but many of us grow up hearing that we do not have what it takes. This strikes at the heart of a man.
#RealMenDontText

Don't make excuses for your boyfriend's joblessness or lack of direction. Excuses don't foster change.
#RealMenDontText

"You have what it takes" is what your man longs to hear. Tell him.
#RealMenDontText

CHAPTER 11

Real Women Give Nice Guys a Chance

chemistry vs. connection

"HE'S JUST NOT WHO I pictured marrying," she said. The words came plummeting out like a confession she'd been harboring for far too long.

"Wait—what do you mean?" I asked, *very* confused.

From where I was sitting, June had met the man she had thought did not exist, and she was head over heels in love. Sam was everything she wanted—I knew this from many conversations and watching her end relationships with others over the years. June had chosen to wait for the right man and had spent many nights alone, wondering if she was making a terrible mistake by not settling for Mr. Good Enough. Then Sam came into her life. June swooned over his daily prayer e-mails to her, his promising career, and how he "just fit" into her family. But this confession didn't add up. I queried further, hoping we could get to the bottom of her conundrum.

"Well, I keep trying to find flaws in him and poke holes in our relationship. He's not tall, dark, and handsome like I pictured. And we don't have that can't-keep-our-hands-off-each-other chemistry. . . ." She paused, then added, "And I've had that with other guys." I could hear guilt in her voice.

Chemistry. Height. Hair color. As we continued to process together, June was able to recognize she had unrealistic expectations for her future husband, as many of us do. She was comparing her boyfriend to—in her words—a cardboard cut-out of Prince Charming. Sam could never compare to this fake Disney icon of husbandly perfection. June had spent years dreaming about Mr. Right, building him up in her head, but the man in her dreams didn't stand a chance in reality.

June's Mr. Right didn't sweep in on a white horse and save her from all her problems. He didn't say, "I wrote you every day for a year. It wasn't over for me. It still isn't over," in the pouring rain. He didn't admit, "You have bewitched me, body and soul—and I love you" against a sweeping backdrop of English countryside. He was five feet eleven (not tall), fair (not dark), and more striking than handsome. He came with baggage—nothing immovable, but baggage they sorted through alongside hers in counseling. He was exactly what she wanted . . . but then he wasn't.

"It's exhausting," she said finally, in tears. "You should see all my pros and cons lists scattered around my car and my office."

June knew she had unrealistic expectations for what marriage should feel like and look like, but this knowledge did

The Man You're Dating
MR. I'M IN A BAND

Mary Ellen has always been attracted to adventurous, spontaneous, May-I-have-this-dance men. So when Dean asks for her number at the local flower shop and casually mentions he'll be on tour for the next couple of weeks, she naturally starts planning their wedding in her mind. A few weeks later, Dean calls—actually calls—and asks if he can take her to dinner. He takes her to a nice dinner, pays for her meal and their bottle of wine, and then drops her off and doesn't even ask to come in! She's sure he's "The One." They start dating, and Mary Ellen thinks the rest will be history. But Dean's band falls apart and so does his self-esteem. The first time he borrows money from Mary Ellen, she doesn't think anything of it. Of course she'd love to help! She's a lawyer and makes a good salary—enough to support them both if Dean would just propose. Two years go by, and Dean has little music jobs here and there, but he is being swallowed by debt.

This situation is difficult, especially when you've invested so much time in a man who is coming unraveled and showing signs he will be more of a burden than an encouragement. Maybe you're dating the man who is still waiting for his "big break" or the one who wants to pursue a creative calling. Quitting a job to be a writer, a musician, or an artist is fine—as long as he has a plan. But if he's floating through life and hopping from one "calling" to the next, you're in for trouble. Get out while you still can!

nothing to stop her from picking Sam apart. How much could she trust her feelings? Should she compare her chemistry with Sam with what she'd had with other men? Did their emotional connection and complementary life paths hold enough weight to support a life together? How could she know if he was right for her?

All good questions—stemming from our culture's confusion about what makes a good relationship and marriage.

When my friend told me that Sam wasn't who she pictured marrying, what she was actually confessing was that he did not complete her. He couldn't. But June eventually realized that a prince on a white horse would also have left her with the familiar feeling that "something was missing." The scary but maybe relieving truth is men were never intended to complete us.

Connection, Anyone?

I recently had a lengthy discussion with my friend Laura about how much chemistry really matters in a relationship. She admitted that while she and her boyfriend of eight months had romantic chemistry, he didn't really "get" her. Making out was easy; deep conversations proved difficult. Her boyfriend was the perfect guy in many aspects—he was driven and had a great job; he was kind and gracious; she loved his family; and they both loved running and traveling. Laura pored over several marriage books attempting to answer her questions: Is it enough for him to be a good, godly man? Does the connection need to be there at the beginning? Her situation is the inverse of June's—she had physical chemistry with her boyfriend but lacked emotional connection. I stared across the table at her, without words, and then she asked, "I mean, you connect with Michael, right? Does deep connection matter in marriage?"

I thought about June and Sam, happily married now with a baby on the way. I have another friend who said she had no chemistry with a man who insistently asked her out—so she set him up with all her friends. Finally, after years of asking, she said yes . . . and one year later they were married. Another friend pictured herself marrying a big executive at her company, so it took years for her to give a local home developer the time of day. They are happily married with two kids. We all know stories where the chemistry went from nonexistent to "Is it your turn to do the dishes or mine?" Even more common are situations where marriages are solely based on chemistry. Suddenly, the feelings evaporate and all that remains is a relationship based on something that doesn't exist anymore. I pleaded the fifth and promised Laura I would mull over her question and talk to Michael that evening.

How much of a role does chemistry play in marriage? What about connection? Is there a difference? How important are they for sustaining a relationship? How do you know if your relationship is based on chemistry? How do you know if he's "The One"?

Chemistry or Connection?

Chemistry is one of those words that is used so often that the meaning can be confusing and muddled. Chemistry is defined as mutual attraction or sympathy, or a reaction, taken to be instinctual, between two persons. The Urban Dictionary defines chemistry as a "mysterious attraction between two people that's out of anyone's control, and either 'just happens' or 'just doesn't happen.'" But where does connection fit in?

Michael and I came up with a definition that may help provide answers to the chemistry/connection conundrum. Chemistry, as we see it, is physical attraction, sometimes intertwined with connection (that's where it gets tricky), that can be present with many different people. I've had chemistry with different boyfriends over the years, even though every one was far from the right man for me to marry. Chemistry is what was behind those nights when you stayed up until 4 a.m. kissing in his car. Chemistry often clouds our vision and lands people in bad marriages. Chemistry is not a necessity in marriage, but more of an added bonus. It can develop over time, especially for women. Since you can have chemistry with many different people, it's not something to say "I do" over.

On the contrary, connection—the feeling that he just gets you on a level that not many people do—is important in marriage. Connection isn't sex; it isn't wanting to jump on top of the other person; and it isn't fireworks. Deep connection grows in marriage instead of waning, like chemistry often does. Connection will keep a relationship strong. This connection is deeper than "we both like *The Office*" or "he makes me feel like a woman." It is true that the sparks—the I can't get enough of you, the need to stay up till 3 a.m. on the phone—will fade. Don't get me wrong; those times still happen every once in a while, but the real spark comes in the day-to-day—for Michael and me, it's how he says he loves me as I walk out the door or how we can dance our troubles away right in our tiny living room.

Michael lived in Germany when we were dating, so I used to call him in the middle of the night, and we'd talk for hours. Recently, I called from California and woke him up, and he answered but said, "I'll talk to you tomorrow, dear." The first time Michael and I kissed, it was like every nerve ending in my body came alive for the first time. It's different now, not because marriage crushes chemistry, but because the chemistry transformed into even deeper connection. And trust me, it's amazing.

I once heard someone say love changing over time is God's way of allowing us to get stuff done—because after some time of four hours of sleep and throwing caution to the wind, you're going to need to pack kids' lunches, actually show up at work on time, and plan for your future. After the chemistry high wears off, you need to be able to connect and make tough decisions and dream about life together.

Chemistry Gone Wrong

When someone asks you about why you love your significant other, think about how you respond. If you find yourself saying something that sounds like, "Oh, we were just made for each other . . . we are just perfect together . . . he makes me feel alive"—and nothing follows, you are probably basing your relationship on a feeling, and feelings don't keep marriages together.

When we fall in love, we tend to lose our grip on reality. I could make a lengthy list of questionable relationships I've been entangled in where everyone (let me rephrase: everyone sober) around me was thinking, *Has she lost her mind?* If you have not experienced one of these relationships based solely on chemistry, then you probably have a friend who has. You know the friend I'm talking about. You roll your eyes when her boyfriend comes around. Whenever you mention one of the many reasons he's all wrong for her, she counters with, "But we are meant to be!" Her parents are wondering how their offspring could possibly be so misguided—and you and other friends are tiptoeing around trying to figure out how to get them to break up. Or perhaps you are the one in a relationship that has others cautioning you about his past and telling you why the relationship has statistically very little chance of surviving. Many people base entire marriages on attraction alone—then suddenly the chemistry experiment explodes, leaving family, finances, and extramarital relationships splattered all over the walls.

Chemistry is how women get a reputation for dating bad boys, players, and deadbeats—and many times the nice guys are left standing on the sidelines. Trust me, I know what this looks like—I dated a guy who sold drugs (one might even use the term "drug dealer") for a few months in college under the I'm-going-to-change-him premise. He gave me diamonds, made me feel beautiful, promised he would change, and said I helped him realize how "lost" he was. Oh, and on occasion he would acquiesce and go to church. Could his feelings for

me transform his drug habit? Could our love win? Absolutely
. . . not.

I've yet to see a situation where a nice girl dated a bad
boy and he became nice too. It just doesn't happen. If he's
headed to the bottom of the ocean with a weight around his
ankle, and you latch on and try to pull him to the surface—
where do you think you'll end up? If most of your friends and
family are rolling their eyes at your relationship, it probably
means you are basing it entirely on chemistry—and it's time
to consider what is at stake. Not just your future, but your
future children's experience of marriage and family.

Get a New List

If you grew up even close to a youth group, you have a list.
Youth groups are notorious for telling teenage girls the consequences of dating around and having premarital sex, and
just what the guy sitting next to them in algebra class is really
thinking. Some give out purity rings as signs of a commitment to wait for their spouses. Others encourage crafting
lists of the qualities they want in their future spouses—to
remind them to wait and not settle for the wrong man or
woman. If you didn't grow up in church, you still probably
have a list of what you want in a husband—maybe shaped
by media, maybe by your friends, or maybe even by your
favorite juicy romance novel. Most of these lists need to be
discarded because the list makers usually don't have the faintest notion of what makes a good marriage.

I most certainly was told to write a list of what I wanted
in a man in the ninth grade. Great concept, but how can a

fifteen-year-old know what she wants or needs in a husband? For the sake of humor, look at what was on my list (I used to go by "Ruth" until the 1,789,343rd person told me it was their very elderly—or worse, dead—relative's name).

Ruth's Future Husband Must . . .

- be a Christian,
- have a good education,
- make me laugh like Megan (my best friend) does,
- be a "cool" Christian—not one of those boring guys (you know the ones I mean),
- play the guitar,
- be sporty and have a good body,
- have read *Redeeming Love*,
- have dark hair and green eyes (I know this is stupid, but it's really important to me, God),
- not think I'm fat,
- like hiking,
- be an adventurer who will travel with me and go running, and
- make me feel good and confident.

My sisters used to say that I'd be able to spot my husband because he'd be standing on the side of the road reading *Redeeming Love* and playing the guitar. I remember writing my list under the impression that if God wants to give us more—abundantly more—than all we ask or imagine, then I should tell him exactly what I want. The problem with the list above, of course, is that as a fifteen-year-old girl with braces and an unhealthy collection of sweater vests, I didn't have the faintest idea of what made a good relationship.

I think we often carry around an immature, high school list shaped by Hollywood when we go groom shopping. You may not have a reading requirement for your Mr. Right, but you probably have a list tucked away in the folds of your brain that dictates your dating decisions. And it may be time to get a new list—especially if your standards are based on a two-dimensional prince.

Instead of shredding your list and widening your parameters on dating sites for an anyone-goes approach, come up with a new list of nonnegotiables for your future spouse. It's vital to set standards so we don't just settle for any guy that checks the church box or makes us feel like the only girl in the room. Walking into a building and sitting in front of a pastor does not make a man a good husband. The real question is whether he will lead your family humbly as a servant—not as a dictator. Or will he be married to his recliner and prefer to sit back instead of engaging with you and your kids?

Standards are important because we have a tendency to major in the minors, don't we? His physique becomes the deal maker, and we overlook his mountain of debt or the wake of angry women behind him. We walk away from stable, secure relationships because someone else makes us laugh more or kisses better—even though Mr. Better Kisser doesn't have a promising future. Relationships are not a checklist by any stretch of the imagination, but it's important to look closely and investigate the things that should be on your list: the qualities that make—or break—a good marriage.

Nonnegotiables

- **Life Direction:** Does his match up with yours? Can you see your life paths intertwining? If he wants to live in the country and own horses, but you've always wanted to live in NYC in a shoe box apartment, this is problematic. Don't start dating and hope to change him.

- **Character:** Remember, the man you marry is the one you'll rely on when you are sick, have a screaming baby, and are too tired to say another word. He will be the father of your children. Is he kind? Does he control and manipulate you? Does he have an anger problem? Again, look at how he treats his mother—this is usually a good indication of the way he will value and treat you.

- **Faith:** If faith is important in your life, he needs to share it. If you are a Christian, the Bible is clear he needs to be a Christian too—not to restrict you from the love of your life, but to save you from the heartache of pulling in the opposite direction from the man you love. It makes life much easier if you are on the same page with who is the boss (i.e., is it God or your bank account?), what moral standards to live by, and what you will teach your kids about eternity.

- **Paycheck:** Not all-important, but since money is the second most common reason for divorce, it's worth mentioning. Does he want to provide for a family? Does he jump from job to job with no clear direction? Be realistic about what you want for your life (if you want four kids, that costs money!) and have the hard conversations before you get engaged. Use some of the tactics in chapter 10 to support your man in this area of his life. On the other hand, money will never make you happy, so don't base your "chemistry" on his hefty paycheck.

- **Friendship:** Do you have fun together? Do you enjoy talking for hours, or do you get bored and just start making out? Do you have a lot in common? If you don't enjoy a wide variety of fun activities together, then marriage will be challenging. Marriage is signing up for a lifetime commitment not just to a spouse, but also to a best friend.

- **Family:** Can you see yourself fitting in to his family and vice versa? Family issues can become huge points of contention in marriage, so it's important to take his (and your) family seriously. Also, how many kids does he want to have? If you want kids, don't marry a man who doesn't, hoping to change him.

This list may help, but I want you to know that a good marriage isn't a paycheck, a picture-perfect family, a "funny personality," or even sitting in a building on Sundays. A good marriage isn't a man who checks all your boxes and has all his ducks in a row. Or even a man with a five-year plan.

A good marriage is a prayer with you in the middle of the night because you can't sleep. A good marriage is someone who is careful with your heart—someone you can trust with your body.

A good man is willing to admit he's broken and needs

Jesus, instead of huffing and puffing and blowing your house down. A man whose kind heart knows that your wardrobe crisis really has nothing to do with your wardrobe and everything to do with you feeling a little insecure. A man to consider marrying is one you know will look into your daughter's eyes and affirm daily that she is beautiful and worthy of love, so she doesn't run to other men to find that affirmation.

The man you want to marry is one who will tell your son it's okay to cry, that Daddy cries, too, laying a hand on his tiny back to cast away shame. A man who will challenge you to soar to the heights and hold you tight when you scrape against rocky terrain. A good marriage is made up of hundreds of inside jokes and all the little moments of ordinary life—toddler wrangling, dirty dishes, and Monday mornings. Good marriages are made of hard work by two parties who are willing to look their selfishness in the eye every single day and surrender it.

I love what Jen Rose wrote at *Good Women Project*:

> The proverbial "One" is someone who will help me
> be holier and more human than I am on my own.
> Not a white knight to rescue me, but a broken, lonely
> wanderer to come alongside and teach my pride to die.
> Someone not to mold me in his image or make me feel
> good, but who will love me enough to let me be myself
> and challenge me to be more than I am.

We don't need rescuing; we need refining. We don't need a parent; we need a partner. We long for companionship, but marriage will not complete us, fix us, or cure us.

Will I Just "Know"?

It's really important to give men a chance—don't say no just because he doesn't make you swoon or you don't immediately start planning your wedding when you first meet him. The first step in giving some nice guys a chance is opening yourself to having coffee with anyone who fits with your new list of nonnegotiable qualities. I mean, really, what is thirty minutes out of your week? If he loves Jesus, has a job, and you are reasonably attracted to him—say yes! Even Hollywood has shown us that the men we never considered can turn out to be Mr. Right (have you seen *Hitch*?).

If after a couple of dates you scrunch your nose at the thought of kissing him, don't waste any more of his time. If he repulses you, then you aren't going to be able to whip up chemistry over time, no matter how furiously you stir. And if you've given him a month or two

text translation 101

PROFESSOR: MICHAEL DEAN

Her: Hey what's up?

Him: Nothing.

Her: I missed you last night. Where did you go?

Him: Beautiful, I'm just not ready for anything serious. I'm so sorry. You're perfect for me, just not right now.

Her: ? But I thought you said you were ready now . . . :(

Him: Naw, not yet. Promise it's not another girl. Just need to get my life together.

Situation: *He tells you he isn't ready for anything serious but promises you he likes you.*

Translation: *A man means what he says in these situations. He isn't ready! Don't hang around waiting for him to be ready. Move on!*

Response: *Don't contact him anymore! If he gets in touch with you, you can let him know you'd like him to stop contacting you because you need to protect yourself from getting hurt.*

of dates and you don't feel a connection, it's probably not going to magically appear. If he just doesn't "get you," it's time to be honest with him and move on. You can't fabricate a deep connection or friendship, no matter how perfect on paper he is for you. Michael's had several friends who tried to do this with women they were dating. Eric dated a girl for six months, always asking, "Am I attracted to her?" Michael finally told him straight up, "Dude, do you want to kiss her? If you even have to think about it, you don't like her." As it turns out, Michael was right. They broke up, and Eric is happily married to someone else now.

If you find yourself in one of these situations where you are ending a relationship or saying no to a second date, please be straightforward and kind. Do not ever go on a date with someone because you feel sorry for him. Think about how you'd feel if a guy asked you out because he felt sorry for you! Kindness always means telling the truth—unless, of course, your mother is asking you if she should invest in wrinkle cream.

How will you know if he's "The One"? Some will say, "You'll just know," but I really do not believe that is true. I thought I'd found "The One" with my two boyfriends before Michael. Michael considered proposing to another girl before he dated me. Dating for a full year before you talk about engagement is typically a good way to discern whether or not he is supposed to be your husband. There is something about spending four seasons with someone that gives clarity. I know couples who went through periods of strong doubts about each other during dating and even engagement who are now happily married, so I don't want you to get the idea that you'll wake up one day and see the writing in the sky: "He's 'The One'!" If you've dated for a year and your feelings are growing stronger, he doesn't have any major red flags, and he meets your nonnegotiables, then it's reasonable to conclude that he's one you could settle down with. But if you've dated for more than eight months and your doubts haven't disappeared, then it's probably safe to walk away. At some point, you just choose to be with that person, no matter what doubts arise.

Brave New World

After experiencing marriage, I now know just how clueless I was before about what makes a good relationship. Like me, you probably want to make the right decision, but it's hard when culture and friends and books are all offering conflicting advice. Because the truth is, marriage is near impossible to predict—you just want to make the best decision possible and know whatever the future holds, you are in it together.

Trying to predict what life will look like in a marriage relationship is similar to guessing what life in a foreign country will entail. Before I moved to China for two years, I took classes, went to seminars about what to expect, talked to others who lived there, read books about Asian living— all to prepare myself for a radical lifestyle change and difficulties that came along with living overseas. While I had read and heard about the crowds and monumental language barriers and dirty streets, that didn't mean I knew what it felt like to get elbowed in the stomach by a lady trying to get on the bus before me, or what it would be like when I asked ninety-seven different salespeople where I could find a "blanket," but the whole time I was saying the word for "cup" (the same word, but it just has a different tone). I didn't know what it would be like to have my picture taken most places I ventured (including the locker room at the gym!) nor what it felt like to have an old man approach me on the street and touch my hair. I could never have been prepared for the enormous challenges I faced there, nor could I have been prepared for the incredible joys that came along with my new home.

I'm standing over here in "Asia" telling you that his dazzling blue eyes or towering height or the way he makes you feel isn't something to build your life on. Marriage is one of the biggest decisions you will make in your life, one that will affect future generations, and it's entirely too easy to base it on all the wrong aspects.

I cannot tell you how small and inconsequential Michael's hair color or height or athleticism or favorite books are in our marriage. The danger of having a Prince Charming cutout stowed away is you might not be able to recognize your guy when he asks you for a date. Your Mr. Right might be the nice guy you've just never considered.

Will you please call your mother and tell her you've decided to start dating nice guys? Maybe she won't need that wrinkle cream after all.

Real Women Give Nice Guys a Chance
In 140 Characters or Less

#RealMenDontText

You can have coffee with anyone. It doesn't mean
you have to marry them.
#chillout #RealMenDontText

Your type might be different than you think.
Give the nice guy a chance.
#RealMenDontText

Trash the Prince Charming cardboard cutout.
He doesn't exist.
#RealMenDontText

Break up with the guy with whom you have
chemistry but nothing more.
#RealMenDontText

Start thinking of marriage as one of the biggest
decisions you will ever make—one that will
also affect your future children.
#RealMenDontText

CHAPTER 12

Real Connection

navigating relationships . . . online

"WHAT DO YOU HAVE to lose by trying it?" he said.

My dignity, I thought, the words sticking in my throat.

It's embarrassing (especially as a six-foot-four man) to admit you are lonely and just want to meet someone . . . and maybe a little desperate, if you are really honest. Online dating made sense, considering I lived overseas, so after much cajoling from friends, I took the plunge. I created a profile, feeling like an idiot—about the same feeling that all of us had the first time we wrote our résumé. *Job history: bag boy at Kroger, and, uh, I mowed the grass every Saturday, and my mom says I'm a hard worker.* You just feel ridiculous pretending you are someone great.

I was apprehensive about signing up for online dating

because I had tried starting a few relationships via Facebook with no success. These interactions were tricky for me because I seemed to have good chemistry with a girl when e-mailing and chatting online, but when we met each other, something was off. It didn't feel like a real relationship; instead, it felt forced. There is something unhealthy about scrolling through a girl's photos night after night and sending messages, hoping you will connect in person.

Funny story? When Ruthie and I talked on the phone for the third time, I felt so self-conscious about my online dating profiles that I told her rather abruptly, "Just so you know, I date online for thirty minutes every morning." After the words left my mouth, I realized I might have just ruined any potential with her and wanted to punch myself in the face. It's a quality I just can't help: I'm honest to a fault. Fortunately she didn't hang up immediately, and my confession was only a minor speed bump. I never did find love online; I closed my eHarmony account a few months later when Ruthie stole my heart.

The stigma attached to online dating even five years ago seems to have vanished as quickly as the phone call. Last year, one in six relationships started online, whether through a traditional dating site or through social media. I know many people who have found amazing relationships online, and others who try to one-up friends with their terrible experiences. Ruthie's friend Lana went to a concert with a guy she met online, and everything went great. He had a job, he was kind, and the conversation flowed. But later that night he started sending her "sexy" pictures of himself posing in

The Man You're Dating
MR. LAST MINUTE

It appears every weekend around the same time: "Hey! What are you up to?" Julie slams her phone down, irritated, but simultaneously excited. Blake texts her a few times during the week with vague intentions for a weekend hangout, but nothing is ever set in stone. This time is no different. Does he expect her to just wait around for him to make up his mind? Julie doesn't want to appear readily available, but she also doesn't want to risk losing the chance to see him. They've been growing closer . . . or so she thinks.

Does this sound like a man on your hands? If he doesn't have time to make plans with you in advance, he's not into you. Men make time for priorities—and unfortunately you aren't one, sister. Move on, and wait for a man who respects you and your time!

his underwear. Disaster. Another friend, Jessica, went to dinner with a guy who showed up in a black-and-red cape. He'd come from work—he was a magician-in-training. Apparently, those capes are difficult to take off. We've heard all the stories, right? To help you avoid racking up any more horror stories for your next girls' night out, I want to use this chapter to discuss best practices for online relationships and dispel any myths about finding love online.

Ready? Make sure you take off your cape before we begin.

E-mail. Talk. Meet.

Ruthie and I are all for meeting online. It's really an excellent way to connect with someone and increase your chances of meeting Mr. Right. We know many great couples who met through online dating sites, blogging, Facebook, and even through witty Twitter banter. Three cheers for how easy the Internet makes finding love.

However, as you probably know from the story of Notre Dame linebacker Manti Te'o and his imaginary girlfriend— or perhaps your own experience—meeting someone online has its pitfalls. We'll discuss these pitfalls and how to sniff out the wrong guys online in this chapter. Meeting someone online may have potential risks, but it doesn't mean you shouldn't safely try to explore this great venue for finding love.

The principles of *Real Men Don't Text* apply to online relationships. If you learn nothing else from this chapter, I want you to understand this simple truth: *Online dating, tweeting, and messaging should always be a vehicle toward a face-to-face relationship, not a replacement. The goal of online connections is to take the relationship off-line.*

Much like texting, online relationships are a pseudo-connection if they remain merely digital. It's not really a relationship if you aren't face to face. We all desire intimacy and connection, and it's sad how many settle for the excitement of online relationships without ever getting to the best part.

E-mail. Talk. Meet. It really is that simple. As a general rule, you want to start by messaging, then talking on the phone, and then meeting. Messaging works well on the online dating sites, but if you connect on social media, then e-mail is best. No texting! If you connect over messages, ask him to set up a time to call. After you've talked on the phone several times, or even for a month, set up a meeting in a public place with an easy exit. Tell a friend where you will be just to be safe. Keep the first meeting to something simple, like coffee, because you don't want to be signed up for a four-hour date when you often know within the first fifteen minutes if it isn't going to work. If he doesn't want to meet, it's the same situation as when a guy isn't willing to substitute his 10 p.m. text for a phone call—time to move on. You want a man who wants to look in your eyes, not just one who scrolls through your pictures.

When You Should (and Shouldn't) Look for Love Online

"How do I know if online dating is for me?" is a common question, because it's really not for everyone. Sometimes there's embarrassment because of the stigma or apprehension about safety. Does it mean you are desperate if you look online? Are you weird for having a "Twitter crush"? Not at all. In fact, I'm going to call you Grandma if you keep waiting for love to drop out of the sky.

Ruthie's friend Shannon recently ended a relationship and immediately jumped into dating online. Within the first week, she had five or six interests, and by the end of the second week, she was communicating with nearly ten different potentials. Great, right? Actually, when it came down to it, she was addicted to the excitement of new relationships and was a bit of a serial dater. When she had a brief lapse between men in the real world, she went to seek this excitement online. *Not good.* You should never jump into online dating to give you a rush, to continue a serial dating pattern, or if you are capital-*D* desperate for love. Desperate women make bad, often dangerous relationship decisions. In the world of online predators, catfishing, and glittery profiles, there is often no room for error. Can we agree that you will examine your motivations and check your boundaries before you jump into dating online? Maybe you aren't ready for that now, but you are ready to work on the deeper issues in your life and find your worth, like Ruthie talked about in chapter 5.

When you are ready, here are some great reasons to look for love online.

- **You have healthy boundaries.** I was committed to not letting the search for love dominate my life. I only allowed myself to get on eHarmony for thirty minutes each morning. I continued to hang out with friends, do my job, travel, run, and meet new people. Make a commitment up front that you won't let online dating take over your life . . . or your thoughts. Have a friend help you keep that commitment.

- **You know the red flags.** We talked about red flags in chapter 7, but we'll also talk about specific red flags to watch out for in online profiles or in first communications.

- **You are committed to safety.** For the first month or two, you will always meet him in a public place and will never get in his car or go to his house. If you have mutual friends (as in real friends, not Facebook friends) that vouch for him, it might be okay to ride somewhere with him or go to his house earlier, but it's generally better to play it safe.

- **Your lifestyle doesn't afford you the chance to meet potentials.** If you work crazy hours, work in an industry with mostly women, or all your friends are married, online dating can be a great way to get yourself out there. When I lived in Germany, I signed up for online dating because I wanted to marry an American and didn't have many chances to meet girls when I was home twice a year. Ruthie's friend Catherine is Chinese, and she signed up for online dating when she moved to the States because she wanted to marry a Chinese man living in the United States. Maybe you just live in a rural community or a small town where there are few options. Hoping love will magically appear is unrealistic. Do something about it!

- **You are tired of meeting guys in bars.** Sign up for online dating or comment on that cute guy's blog you love! Bars can be the worst places to meet guys, because the truth is that most are just looking for a lady for tonight. And you're a forever kind of girl.
- **You are sick of the church dating scene.** "Meet someone at church," my mentor used to tell me, but churches can often be pressure cookers for relationships. If you go to church and haven't found love, why not try taking the pressure off and making yourself available online? You never know what can happen!

Don't be ashamed. Get out there! Technology has made relationships tricky, but let's embrace technology for its benefits, too. But before you do, let's look at some red flags that warn of danger ahead.

Red Flags When Meeting Online

When online dating, here are some red flags to look out for on guys' profiles and in your initial interactions that will save you time and perhaps tears down the road.

- **He wants to meet you right away.** No guy should be beating down your door upon meeting you online. If he seems obsessed right away, this is a huge danger sign. Just say no. Now, if you have mutual friends, work at the same company, or there is some other

reason why it's safe to meet right away, there might
be an exception. Otherwise? Tell him you aren't
interested.

- **He pressures you.** If you aren't ready to meet, you aren't
ready. If you don't want to be exclusive, that is your pre-
rogative. What do you want? Answer this question for
yourself, and don't apologize to anyone. If a guy tries to
pressure you to do something you are uncomfortable
with in the first month of dating/meeting, just imagine
how bad it will be down the road.

- **He displays anger or extreme emotion.** This is an
early sign of an emotionally abusive person. Please
be careful; there are no excuses for anger or intense
emotions in profiles, online, or over the phone before
you've met. If you don't want to continue dating or
communicating with someone, you don't owe him an
apology or an explanation.

- **He sends you a "sexy" picture.** These pictures can
be anything from shirtless to naked. Huge red flag—
it's not cute, it's not funny, it's not sexy. Stop all
communication.

- **He asks concerning questions.** I've heard it all. Any
questions that raise an eyebrow probably mean you
need to run. Close the communication with him
immediately. Some examples I've heard: "Would you
cut your hair for me?"; "Would you be my slave for
a week if I asked you to?"; "Would you have sex with
my friend if I asked?"; "How committed are you to
staying below 130 pounds?"; "Will you send me a

picture of your breasts?"; "Let's get drunk and see where it takes us, okay?"; "Will you come over?"

- **He reveals inconsistent information about himself.** Have you heard of catfishing? A catfish is someone who creates a false identity using Facebook or other social media, particularly to pursue deceptive online romances. Inconsistent information is an indicator that the person on the other end may not be at all who they portray.

- **He sends messages that seem like form letters.** "Hey, sexy! Your profile caught my eye like no one's ever has ;)" . . . One word: NO! Don't fall for this message that he's probably sent to ten others tonight. If it sounds like boilerplate, don't respond.

- **He compliments your physical appearance the first time he contacts you.** You don't want a man who is only into you because of what you look like or someone who is overly appearance focused. He shouldn't be noting (out loud) how hot you are right in the beginning.

- **He has lists of dos and/or don'ts in his profile.** This is a sign of someone who is demanding and bitter, neither of which I'm guessing you want in a mate. Don't respond, don't answer, and don't meet. Examples? "She must be fit, know how to cook, be open to the wild side of the bedroom." Yikes.

- **He won't talk on the phone.** Huge red flag. Stop responding to his messages. What legitimate reason could he have for not wanting to talk to you?

- **He puts off meeting you for an unrealistic period of time.** One word: catfish. Don't listen to one more excuse. Get out!

- **He overshares.** The Internet is not the place for you to find out about his ex-wife, his heartache from his last relationship, the mistakes he's made, or his childhood wounds. Those conversations need to happen face-to-face—but not on the first date.

- **He makes you feel sorry for him.** If you find yourself feeling guilty—or he tries to make you feel guilty—for not being into him, returning his calls, or doing as he asks, this is a major red flag. Move on! Don't base a relationship on feeling sorry for someone—and never, ever should I catch you on a pity date. He doesn't need your sympathy!

- **He references past relationships early on.** This is a sign he's not over his exes. You are not a rebound girl!

text translation 101

PROFESSOR: MICHAEL DEAN

Him: Great to meet you!

Her: You too! Such a small world.

Him: We should get dinner sometime.

Her: I'd like that. :)

Him: How about next weekend?

Her: I'd love to. Call me maybe? haha

Situation: He meets you at a party/social gathering and texts you afterward to say hi or something sweet like "Wonderful to meet you last night!"

Translation: He is probably interested, but it's too early to know anything about him. Don't raise your hopes too high, and wait and see if he actually calls.

Response: You can text back, but after a few texts end the conversation and ask him to give you a call sometime. Or suggest a time for him to call.

- **He makes plans and cancels or is sporadic in communication.** Unfortunately, not-quite-single or even married men are online trolling for women. Canceled plans or sporadic communication might mean he is relationally unavailable. Be smart and trust your gut.

Finally, my friends, don't get too attached online. You need to remember that this, like face-to-face dating, is a way to see if he is the right man for you. Also, you have many options online—and so does he. A match declining you or not responding to communication can be hurtful, so try to maintain a healthy view of yourself and not place your worth in how many guys are interested. That's another reason I recommend having a set amount of time each week for online dating—so it doesn't start to define you or take over your life. Try to see it more like sports practice rather than the National Championship with three seconds left in the game.

FAQs about Online Relationships

- **How do I enhance my profile?** NO SELFIES (self-taken pictures) EVER. Ask a friend to take pictures of you. I automatically closed matches that had these pouty-face, I-have-really-long-arms pictures. I was always wary of girls who seemed self-obsessed.
- **What should I never put on my profile?** How much you make, where you live, your measurements, or a wide age range. Stick to plus or minus five years from your age.

- **Do I even have a chance of finding a good man online?** Yes, absolutely! There is a guy out there who, like me, was ready and willing to take a step of faith and try online dating. Even if you try it and don't meet someone, it's not a waste of time or money, because you are getting practice. Dating doesn't come naturally!

- **What should I look for in an online dating service?** Use a big-name dating service, not a smaller, cheaper one, because those don't necessarily attract the type of guys you are looking for. With online dating, you get what you pay for; sites that are free generally attract people who aren't taking it seriously or who are just looking for a hookup.

- **If I am a Christian, should I only stick to Christian dating sites?** Not necessarily. Most quality dating services get to know what's important to you, and if your faith is a large part of that, it will come through on your profile. In fact, I've heard some horror stories from solely Christian or Jewish sites, so don't stick with ChristianMingle or JDate because you think it's safer.

- **Is it okay to date multiple guys simultaneously?** Sure! But do periodic check-ins to make sure you aren't building a list of suitors just to feel better about yourself. Widening your options and communicating with and even seeing several guys simultaneously can be a great way to protect yourself and not get attached too soon.

- **How much should I reveal about myself in my profile?**
  Remember, revealing more will not always attract more
  men. You need to make sure to leave some mystery.
  When I saw a profile that was too lean, I would think
  the girl wasn't taking it seriously, but if it was really
  long, I didn't want to sift through all of it to look for
  something that interested me.

There are thousands of success stories out there of people
meeting and falling in love over the Internet. Ruthie's good
friend Kayla met her now husband through a Twitter conversation that quickly led to Skyping and then to meeting. Many
of my friends have dated and found love online. Technology
can really mess up relationships, but on the flip side, if you are
smart and know the common pitfalls, red flags, and who you
are looking for, technology can be a great matchmaker. Just
make sure all your efforts are leading to a good, old-fashioned
face-to-face relationship. Happy dating!

Real Connection
In 140 Characters or Less

#RealMenDontText

The goal of online connections is always to take the
relationship off-line.
#RealMenDontText

You want a man who wants to look in your eyes,
not just one that scrolls through your pictures.
#RealMenDontText

You might be a good candidate for online dating
if: Your lifestyle doesn't afford you the chance
to meet potentials.
#giveitashot #RealMenDontText

Churches can be pressure cookers for relationships.
Why not take the pressure off and try dating online?
#RealMenDontText

Know the red flags in meeting online, proceed with
caution, but have fun! It's a great way to meet someone.
#RealMenDontText

CHAPTER 13

Real Women, Messy Bedrooms, and Hope

when you're desperate for more

BEFORE MICHAEL AND I MARRIED, my idea of cooking a gourmet meal was to pop a veggie burger and some frozen vegetables in the microwave. I'd envisioned learning to cook when I married, but marriage felt more like a distant dream than something that would actually come to fruition. By way of disclaimer for the feminists, I must mention I wanted to learn to cook not because I embrace traditional gender roles, but because I love the way a home-cooked meal warms Michael's heart. Anyway, I wasn't really self-conscious about my lack of cooking expertise, because I thought that once I got married, my love for my husband would transform my lackluster desire to be in the kitchen. *Oh, I was wrong.*

The Sunday evening after our honeymoon, Michael and I

were doing the newlywed "polite dance," as I call it, trying to figure out how to live together and where to put all our stuff. I'd venture to say I was kinder back then, merely suggesting that Michael's framed print of him doing a flip off a cliff might look better tucked away in our extra bedroom rather than our living room. Or that while I appreciate an outside-the-box thinker, a football on our couch didn't exactly work in the place of a throw pillow.

Naturally, it was the perfect moment to pull out my recipe book and commence learning to cook. I mean, how hard could following a recipe really be? While I was busy browning the turkey sausage, I asked my sweet husband if he wouldn't mind cutting up the onions and garlic. He began cutting as I instructed, "One cup of chopped onions and three cloves of garlic, minced." He chopped, I browned, the football and cliff-jumping picture were not in the living room—marriage was easy peasy. I tossed everything in the Crock-Pot, proud of myself for mastering my first recipe, and went to bed.

The next day, I walked in from work expecting a house filled with the aroma of Cuban black bean deliciousness proclaiming my excellent wifery, but instead, all I smelled was *garlic*. I opened the Crock-Pot and peered inside, wondering what had gone wrong. *What in the world have I done? Is this how it's supposed to smell?*

Then a faint memory of cooking with my mom came to the forefront, and I knew just what had happened. "Hey, Michael! Does a clove of garlic mean the whole head or just one of the little sections?"

We nearly fell on the floor in tears of laughter as the thick, non-sexy aroma of garlic hung over our very small kitchen. "So I put more like twenty cloves of garlic in our soup!" Michael said. After I proceeded to burn the bread, setting off the fire alarm, he suggested going out to dinner the next several nights to "take the pressure off" me. He's a smart man.

My cooking ability in marriage (or lack thereof) could have easily been predicted by looking at my past cooking experience, but for some reason I was surprised that I did not morph into a gourmet cook after returning from our exotic honeymoon. I had a new last name, new husband, and new house; but at the end of the day, I was still the same passionate, determined noncook who was messy at times, stubborn at least six and a half days a week, and left clothes everywhere when I went to work. To be honest, I was also surprised I wasn't kinder, gentler, or at least a little less selfish—because we had prepared for marriage.

As comical as the cooking story is, I share it because I want you to think about how much easier learning to cook is than, say, beating a ten-year battle with sex addiction or working through unresolved childhood issues. Of course I wouldn't magically transform into the perfect cook or neatest roommate, but I believed marriage would erase the areas of my life I wanted to change.

Amanda believed her weight problem would disappear in marriage because her spouse would help her eat healthy and avoid junk food. Mary Grace had the worst time waking up in the morning and was often late for work and other important engagements. She thought marriage would bring respite from the havoc her oversleeping problem brought to her life because her early morning husband would help her. Sari thought being able to finally have sex would fix her tendency to watch porn late at night.

Fast-forward to one year into marriage. Amanda's food issues are nearly sending her husband over the edge because he doesn't know how to help her. Mary Grace's sleep problems are now affecting not just her life but the life of her husband, and she still can't get up unless Caleb forces her to get out of bed. Sari still watches porn on occasion after her husband goes to bed, and he has no idea why she's lost interest in sex. Meeting the right man will not fix us.

Culture will tell you marriage will wipe away your past, but it doesn't. Marriage will never fix your lust problem, or his lust problem; your selfishness, or his selfishness. Most marrieds I talk to remark how many of their issues are not lessened but heightened because we live day in, day out in such a close relationship with our spouses. It's true for Michael and me—and will be for you, too.

The past is the best predictor of the future. If you are a hot mess now, not even a perfectly planned wedding will change anything about your tendency to live in stress and chaos. If you have a very dark closet full of childhood secrets, they will show up in your marriage. If you numb your feelings with alcohol now, you are going to head straight for the liquor cabinet when your husband upsets you. Do you tend to rail at people for the smallest faults? Your anger will rip your marriage apart— because I promise you will blow up at your spouse way more than you can imagine. If you are a classic overspender, unwilling to be bothered with words like debt and savings—this

The Man You're Dating
MR. LATE NIGHT

Cara's relationship with Freddy all started from a last-minute text message: "Can you meet me downstairs in 20?" He wanted to take her to a party, and she knew it was her big chance to make an impression. She was under the covers but got out of bed to get ready and meet him downstairs. She admitted she should have said no to his late-night, last-minute text, but she didn't want to lose her big shot at dating a guy she'd swooned over for two years. They did start dating, but it was miserable. For eight months Cara made constant excuses for her "boyfriend" and actually started taking medicine to curb her anxiety about their relationship and his inconsistency. When they were together, it felt right—the chemistry was intoxicating. And one day he just broke it off. It took her a year to recover from the breakup.

If he is interested in more than just a convenient girl, he'll contact you during Starbucks hours, not during sex hours. Don't fall for the lines that he misses you, he can't live without you, or he needs you. The only thing he needs is to be removed from your phone.

habit may destroy your marriage. Meeting the right man, planning the perfect wedding, and making promises to each other doesn't change one ounce of who you are. After the wedding bells are quiet and the dance floor empty, neither your new last name nor the great man you married is going to change your habits, your tendencies, or your addictions. As the saying goes, "Wherever you go, there you are."

But it's not the end. You can start breaking habits in your life now that are destructive to future relationships. You can become the good woman the right man is looking for. You don't have to settle for text messages, hookups, or dating the space-filler guy. What you do now, whether you are fifteen or forty-five, matters. Instead of focusing all your energy on meeting the right man, why not divert some attention and focus on becoming the right woman?

How many of you are thinking that your greatest relationship problem is you just haven't met the right man yet? It may be true, but might it be possible that you are not ready for the right man? If Mr. Right walked into the room this minute, would he be drawn to you?

He's Not Looking for You

I recently heard a story that demonstrates why you want to be preparing for a great marriage now. Laura moved to Atlanta, where she started putting her standards and priorities on the back burner to make way for a more "dynamic" social life, if you will. She still wanted marriage and didn't give up her faith, but she decided she just wanted to have fun for a few years. So she and her friends had their fun—and in the midst of it all she met this incredible man at a Christmas party. He was the man who hugged kids in church and built houses for those less fortunate on the weekends; she left completely smitten, thinking that he might just be "The One." Laura spent the next week talking to her roommate, Michelle, about him, until finally Michelle looked at her and said, "The problem is a guy like that isn't looking for a girl like you . . . or me. I'm sure he's not spending the night with different women, and he's not looking for someone who has a new man every weekend." Laura excused herself and cried, knowing Michelle was right. She had put her marriage dreams on hold in the name of wanting to have fun now. The "amazing, perfect guy" never called or pursued Laura. She wasn't the woman he was looking for. Maybe two years ago she had been, but she had traded in her desire to be with the right guy for a desire to be with someone right now. Laura was devastated and vowed to live differently.

I know what it feels like to think a certain man or relationship will fix our brokenness, but relationships don't change people; they only direct the spotlight on areas of weakness. In single life, we can put all our issues, selfish tendencies, and occasional habits behind closed doors, in sealed boxes. If a friend comes too close to our wounds, we can write her off and make new friends. If our boyfriend threatens to open our secret boxes, we can leave him. But in marriage those doors get flung wide open and the boxes get dumped out—usually all over our spouse. And we're stuck. That's why the divorce rate is where it is and why affairs, pornography, debt, and broken relationships are choking good marriages.

What you are doing now will show up in your future relationships. Even if you're just seventeen, it matters. Your past becomes your future. Let's look at an example.

Jenny is the classic girl next door. She works as a high-powered consultant and is highly desired by a number of suitors. In a world where it feels like no one is dating, she is consistently asked out by different guys. But Jenny has high standards, and it's rare that she gives a guy more than one date. Even though she started having sex in high school, she is now committed to saving sex for marriage.

Jenny meets a local artist named Jake; they fall in love and get married. Happily ever after, right? A year or two into marriage, Jenny and Jake are wondering what went wrong. Jake feels threatened by Jenny's charm and vibrant social life—and Jenny starts to think she married the wrong guy because he "isn't any fun." They seek counseling after Jenny comes home drunk one night at 3 a.m. with a note in her purse that simply says, "I've never met anyone like you. Call me." Jake is livid and Jenny is defensive. "It's not like anything happened! Get over yourself. I was just having fun and didn't do anything wrong." Jenny and Jake see a counselor and discover they've both been living as married singles. Jenny thought Jake's love and the commitment of marriage would "fix" her desperation for attention—but when Jake became consumed in his art business, she sought attention elsewhere. She justified the late nights downtown and flirty run-ins because "she wasn't doing anything." She wasn't having an affair, just a good time. Jenny continued to justify her "good times" until eventually she kissed a man at her office.

Jake grew more bitter and distant, until he didn't feel like he loved her anymore.

Okay, confession time—I'm a lot like Jenny. Five years ago I realized my flirtatiousness and need to be desired by every guy in the room wasn't going to disappear just because the right guy came into my life. Those lapses in judgment where I made out with a bartender from work or the guy on the trip I took around China represented a pattern in my life that needed to be worked through before I would be able to attract a good man. Even if I did attract a good man, I would bring my craving for attention into our marriage—and possibly elsewhere when my husband didn't meet my "needs." As I've said before, our tendency to date losers, to need the attention of every man in the room, or to settle for the wrong man is always a symptom of a deeper problem. My "mess-ups" were evidence of a deeper lack of self-worth. I took a year off dating and worked on being confident in myself apart from what men were or weren't saying about me. Not easy, but necessary.

Ready for another confession? I have some issues stemming from childhood pain that I knew would only be highlighted in marriage. I can be defensive and extremely sensitive. I've seen this side of me surface in several conversations with Michael. Like the time he simply said, "Chicken on the bone isn't my favorite," and I burst into tears, declaring how hard I try and what a terrible wife I'd become. He just sat wide eyed, assuredly thinking, *All I said was this meal wasn't my favorite.* For you, it may be anger issues, unresolved childhood pain, unforgiveness, a lack of responsibility—but we all have issues. It's what you do to prepare to be Mrs. Right that can make all the difference. Before Michael and I married, I did a significant amount of counseling to help work through the past in order to ensure I didn't respond to Michael in an unfair way. It's easy to transfer our pain onto our spouses without even realizing why we're reacting in such an extreme manner.

Marriage will not fix you, change you, or heal your deepest wounds. Will you take this message to heart and start preparing for marriage *now*? I want to help you not just wait for and find the right man, but also prepare to stay married no matter what storms beat against your life. The past does not have to be your future, because there is something much better, much deeper, much higher than all of these relationships.

The Big Six

Let's look at six big areas that need special attention before marriage. We're focusing on you here, but it goes without saying that these issues apply to the man you're dating too. Please do not fall into the predictable pattern where you believe you can change a man and he ends up changing you.

- **Unresolved childhood issues:** It's vital for the health of your future marriage that you start working through your childhood, especially if you experienced a broken family, sexual abuse, or violence in the home. These issues determine how you are triggered to respond in similar situations or with similar emotions. Start seeing a counselor now. Great books? *Breaking Free* by Beth Moore and *The Wounded Heart* by Dan B. Allender. Also, if you have a difficult relationship with your dad, *Abba's Child* by Brennan Manning is a great resource.

- **Unforgiveness:** If you are quick to write people off or have a string of broken relationships marked by unforgiveness in your past, it's important to consider how this part of your character will affect your marriage. It's common to think the right man will never make us as angry or as hurt as others have, but I can promise you he will. Good marriages are built on forgiveness, because the man you marry will do things that make you wild with anger and sadder than you can imagine feeling. I also should note that forgiveness does not mean lying on the floor and welcoming someone to beat you up again. It doesn't mean you ignore the past and pretend that this person will not hurt you again or you say the pain he caused you wasn't real. Rather, it lets the person off the hook, declaring, "You don't owe me anything." As Anne Lamott says, "Not forgiving is like drinking rat poison and then waiting for the rat to die." A couple of great books to read are *Safe People* by Henry Cloud and John Townsend and *Choosing Forgiveness* by Nancy Leigh DeMoss.

- **Selfishness:** Six months after we got married, our premarital counselors asked Michael and me the one thing that surprised us most about marriage. We both said, "Selfishness." Well, actually Michael first said, "Toothpaste" (I'm a messy toothpaste user) and then selfishness. Marriage highlights selfishness; so if you still want your single life, don't get married. Marriage is designed to be a partnership—and it takes work! Prepare yourself to have your world turned upside down in marriage, by slowly starting to be more flexible in your lifestyle. You'll have to make many compromises, so start now. Practice kindness and consideration of others.

- **Pornography:** It's no longer just a man's battle. Studies have shown that 40 percent of women struggle with pornography.[1] Some Christian women have told me they thought getting married and being able to have sex would fix their porn problem. But you could talk to one thousand porn watchers and find that's never the case. The reason you are looking at porn has almost nothing to do with lust, but everything to do with past trauma, insecurities, anxiety, or fear . . . and a desire for God. The absolute best book I can recommend on this subject is *Surfing for God: Discovering the Divine Desire beneath Sexual Struggle* by Michael John Cusick. Please don't wait any longer to work on this addiction that will not be left behind with your maiden name. You can't promise or pray your way out of it.

- **Spending habits:** Money is often cited as one of the top two reasons for divorce. Before marriage, you need to pay off all your debt and start living

---

1. "Infographic—Porn Addiction in America," Porn Harms Research, August 13, 2012, http://pornharmsresearch.com/2012/08/infographic-porn-addiction-in-america-statistics/.

responsibly. Dave Ramsey's Financial Peace University is a great way to avoid financial pain down the road. If you've never had a savings account—you spend all your extra money on clothes or eating out—then you aren't mature enough to get married. Develop some healthy financial patterns now to prepare to meet the right man. A mountain of debt is a huge turnoff, not to mention a terrible way to live.

- **Fantasy relationships:** Flirting and addiction to male attention also falls in this category. Marriage will not satisfy your need to be noticed, because your husband cannot fill this void. If you struggle with fantasy relationships, seek counseling and learn to combat these thoughts before marriage. Also, Andy Stanley's *Guardrails* series online is a must-watch to set healthy boundaries in marriage.[2]

Marriage Is(n't) the Answer

"We're getting married!" she shouted in my ear over the phone.

"Wait . . . what?"

"Tim proposed! I know it's fast, but it just feels so right."

Lynn was not the first girl who thought her entire life was leading to the moment where she'd meet Mr. Right and live happily ever after. She and Tim had only dated for six months—and they'd started dating two weeks after Lynn had spent a week drinking and confessing her love to her ex-boyfriend. She was a serial dater and seemed to consistently

---

2. You can watch the videos online at http://www.northpoint.org/messages/guardrails.

have a long line of men who wanted to be hers. Unfortunately, relationships like Lynn and Tim's have a predictable pattern. Infatuation leads to marriage; marriage grows difficult when the infatuation wears off and both parties resort to their past tendencies . . . and distant marriage or even divorce looms.

When you rely on men or marriage to solve your deepest insecurities or character flaws, you will always be let down. The right man will never fix you no matter how much you desperately want to be the right woman for him. I know this truth might feel hopeless, but I'm standing here telling you there is hope. Your messy bedroom, failed dreams, or broken relationships are never the end.

The Talk

I was nearly shaking when we had the conversation.

Michael and I had reached the point in dating where we needed to talk about past relationships. I was terrified to tell him about my past because, in my book, he was perfect. He exemplified character and purity, and I felt so unworthy of his love. It was like I'd been plugging holes in the walls of my heart, but suddenly it would burst from the pressure and the secrets. After trying to start the conversation in twelve different ways, I blurted it out: "I've messed up . . . a lot. My dating life has been far from pure." While Michael was praying for his future wife, I was lying to my parents about my boyfriends or kissing guys outside parties or bars. What felt devastating to me was that while Michael had been waiting patiently with me in mind, I had been getting as close as I could to the edge without falling off.

I held my breath, waiting for Michael's response, and the tears started to flow. He put his hand on my face and said something eloquent that ended with, "You aren't that girl anymore. Not even close. Your past does not define you." He was right. I wasn't the same woman anymore, but I still felt my past cast a shadow on the truth of who I really was. But when Michael looked at me, he saw a beautiful woman who loved women so deeply sometimes it hurt—not the high school or college girl dating a string of bad guys. What a grace-filled man I married.

If in reading this book you have felt judged for your past or hopeless about your future because you've done it wrong, this feeling was far from our intention. The truth is you can have another shot at getting this right—no matter if it's your second, fifth, or twenty-seventh chance. Maybe you believe you don't deserve a good man because of your past. Perhaps you've fallen into the lie that God is punishing you—cruelly dangling marriage in front of you. Or maybe you believe you are too long gone, too screwed up, too old, too unattractive to ever find a good man. Michael and I believe in a bigger plan, a bigger story, than statistics or your failures. So keep reading, dear sister. Your future is full of hope and bright possibilities.

Real Life Change

"100 Reasons Why I Like You"—the e-mail subject line that popped up on the screen was enough to make Annie stop and nearly squeal in anticipation. The e-mail was from her boyfriend, John.

"I like how incredibly intelligent you are. I like how your intelligence is coupled with amazing humility. You're beautiful. I miss your smile right now, and I just saw it yesterday. . . ." Annie's boyfriend listed reason after reason why he liked her. He liked her hugs and their "seat back" late-night car conversations. After listing ninety-nine reasons why John liked Annie, he'd typed out the words "I can imagine a future with you."

What every woman dreams will happen . . . one day.

Annie had to pinch herself to believe this was really happening to her. "A godly, handsome man likes one hundred things about me?" She giggled through our entire phone conversation later.

Five years before she received this e-mail, Annie had ended a relationship she thought would result in marriage. She had been a serial dater of wrong men. After becoming a Christian, she learned that she needed a major overhaul of who she was as a woman and with whom she was looking to spend her life, so she broke up with her boyfriend. But Annie was terrified her past would keep God from giving her a husband. She was wracked with guilt over her sexual history.

Over the next five years, Annie and I had many conversations about dating and relationships. I weighed in on her bad relationships, sympathized with her distress as friends were married around her, and listened as she lamented that she'd never meet someone. One night over dinner, Annie looked at me across the table and said, "You ruined my life. If it weren't for you, I'd be married with a baby now." If I'm honest, her comment terrified me. I wondered if I should have just kept my thoughts to myself and let her marry a man I knew was wrong for her—because then at least she'd be married. It can be frightening to tell the truth to friends we love. Was it even truth? Or had I gotten it all wrong?

At the end of those five years, Annie started dating an amazing man—and the joy of being in the right relationship and finding respect for herself far outweighs a few years of singleness. Listen to what she writes:

What if everything I did in dating was wrong? I wish I had a better story to tell you, perhaps that I have never messed up before or I'm happily married with kids. But I don't.

I grew up not knowing much about dating and relationships, and I went to college at sixteen. I was abused and assaulted. These experiences took away my innocence and twisted my view on sex and marriage into a dirty and hopeless reality. I imagined ending up as a single mom with kids, not knowing who their fathers were. Sounds dramatic, but I felt I was bad at my core. I separated sex and love and began to use sex to gain temporary happiness and comfort, to numb the pain and stress, and also as a way to ask for help.

As I protected myself with the lie that sex is just physical, my shell grew thicker and thicker. I felt dark and worthless of love. I did not believe I could ever break out of this never-ending cycle.

But then I met a friend who loves me and introduced me to God's love. Could God love someone

as screwed up as me? Yes, he could! I finally realized
I had been looking for the unconditional love and
forgiveness God promises.

I broke up with my boyfriend, and the next five
single years sometimes made me wonder if God was
punishing me. Looking back, those five years, albeit
painful, were critical to my growth and healing. Just
recently, God brought a gentle, understanding, and
godly boyfriend to me. He has helped me continue to
walk the journey—through the pain and shame and
toward healing. There is hope. There are shame and
scars, but God is working in my life to bring healing to
me every day. The defenses borne out of the hurts from
both our pasts continue to cause us to hurt each other,
but there is hope. Wherever God takes this relationship,
we are both convinced that God will complete the
great work that he has started in us and continued
throughout this frustratingly wonderful past year of
dating. And so we learn, we love, and we grow.

If you have messed up even terribly before and feel
your relational life is hopeless, I long for you to find
hope—strong hope—not in the person you are dating,
but in God. Nothing is impossible. Even though the
healing process is painful, it is real and draws the best
and worst of us out to rely on God. There is hope.
Don't ever forget!

I hope you'll remember Annie's and my stories when you
are tempted to go over to his house *just one more time*, or go

back to your ex when you feel lonely, or lower your standards this once. In addition, it should be noted that neither Annie nor I changed while simultaneously dating Mr. Wrong . . . or Mr. Right. It took us years to learn the truth about ourselves, reprogram our dating patterns, and be able to recognize the good men. Years coupled with hard work.

What Now?

Depending on how drastic an overhaul your relational decisions warrant, you may need to take a break from men altogether. A wave of responsible dating will not fix the patterns in your life and heart created from casual sex and long-term detrimental relationships. You need time to sort out your past and reprogram your mind. I've heard experts recommend circling a date on the calendar that's a year from now and committing to not date for an entire year. This commitment will take a great deal of resolve but will set you up well for the future. After a major slip with a guy just three weeks before I left for China, I took a year off

text translation 101

PROFESSOR: MICHAEL DEAN

Him: Got plans for the weekend?

Her: I'm sort of old fashioned and usually don't make dates over text messages. I'd love to go out with you, I'd just ask you to call :)

Him: Of course, talk to you soon!

(Her phone rings.)

Situation: You meet a really nice guy through mutual friends, and he follows up with a text message.

Translation: Take a deep breath—he's probably interested in you but just doesn't know your standards yet.

Response: Explain to him gently that it is okay to call you, and if he is really interested he will. He should respond accordingly.

dating, and it was a great way to find my worth, learn to respect myself, and reprogram my mind in regard to dating. Otherwise, I can only imagine I'd still be dating in my old pattern and gritting my teeth trying to fix myself. A year off dating might be exactly what the doctor ordered.

How do you get a second chance at relationships? How do you swap your view of yourself as "messed up" or "slutty" or "too old" with the truth of who you are? What if you've already had sex . . . now what? How do you make sure your past does not destroy your future? I want to give you five practical steps to start changing your future today.

- **Stop having sex.** Make a commitment to wait until you are married. It doesn't matter how many sexual partners you've had or how hard it will be to explain your newfound commitment to your boyfriend or fiancé, you need to stop having sex in order to gain clarity about relationships. Purity brings clarity about whether or not you should be together. If you are living with your boyfriend, move out. You can't keep repeating the past and expect the future to be different.

- **End your text-based relationships.** If irresponsible texting is too tempting, take text messaging off your phone to ensure you don't have to read this book again the next time you hit that place where you realize the man texting you is putting forth zero effort and getting everything from you. For many of you, texting is only getting you into trouble and putting

you in compromising relationships. Rid yourself
of this temptation!

- **Surround yourself with better friends.** This is a big
one. Many women resolve to date differently but
slide back into old habits because they keep the same
friends—friends who continually encourage and
model poor dating decisions. If you are the only one
trying to make a change, it is going to be hard to
do it alone. Surround yourself with people who will
encourage you. If all your friends are living with guys,
sleeping around, texting several guys—you may need
to get new friends. You may be strong enough to keep
these friends and make others, but I advise you to
think critically about whether or not you can do this
and still make tough decisions, ones your old friends
will not be encouraging. Regardless, try to make a few
friends to hold you to the standards you've set.

- **Find a married mentor—and emulate her.** Ask her
questions about her relationships, her mistakes, what
has worked well, how she figured out waiting for sex,
and anything else you need to know. Give her permission to ask you hard questions about dating, such as
"Are you spending more time talking or kissing?" or
"Will he be a good father to your children?"

Learning to date differently is hard work, just like breaking any other habit in your life. You need a new mind and
heart. It may take avoiding places like bars and clubs where
you have a tendency to meet the wrong guys. It may mean

not even kissing your boyfriend because the temptation to keep sleeping together is too strong. It may mean not dating for two years while you work on yourself. You may need to remove text messaging from your phone and end all your dates by midnight. Be smart about what you can and can't handle. When I was trying to date differently, I still let myself be in many compromising situations with men, telling myself the lie that I could handle just talking and then go home. You may have more self-control than I did, but I have a feeling I'm pretty normal. Make tough decisions now for a better future. And no more lying to yourself!

Messy Bedrooms

Wherever you are in your faith journey, please know that Michael and I care about you and accept you exactly as you are. We are far from "perfect Christians" and don't have a hidden agenda in this book. It's not a line, and it's not a bait and switch to try to change you. As someone who took years to recover from some painful experiences in the church, I understand apprehension about the whole idea of Jesus. The message of Christianity is often muddled by how "church people" conduct themselves, and Jesus really needs some new PR. If you've felt forced into a box, or even hated by Christians, please allow me to apologize. It was never the way Jesus intended you to be treated.

Michael and I just can't finish these last few chapters without sharing our story and this amazing life we've found through forgiveness. We've found a wide-open door to a different life, a new life, one where we don't have to drag our pasts behind us. If Jesus really is as great as we believe he is, we think it would be selfish to keep it to ourselves. You can skip the next section if you feel uncomfortable, okay? No agenda. Just sharing life.

Men or perfect relationships or marriage or good self-esteem cannot fix us—we need more than dating strategies and the willpower to live differently. New Year's resolutions and fasts from dating can solve a tiny piece of the problem—but can't ultimately change our hearts. When I refused to touch Christianity with a ten-foot pole, I was protecting myself from the judgment I experienced from church people. I wanted to live how I wanted without their critical eyes and shaking fingers, and that is exactly what I did. I partied, dated who I wanted, and drank myself into oblivion every weekend. "Living it up" for me actually turned out to be miserable and empty, a feeling of Novocain seeping into my veins and dulling the cries of my soul. I couldn't pinpoint exactly what was wrong; it just all felt terrible. I had moments when I wanted to disappear.

When my social decisions started to wreck my life, I thought I could simply decide to live differently and my life would stop unraveling. But that just wasn't the case. I stopped drinking, but then I couldn't stop basing my worth on men. I stopped dating, but then I couldn't cease turning to food for comfort. I stopped using food as a vice and slipped back into dating all sorts of losers. No matter how shiny I looked on the outside—my academic achievements, my attractiveness, or my vibrant social life—I felt like hopelessness was slowly eating its way through my heart. I was desperate for something more than all of this. Was Jesus the only answer?

He was the only way I could forgive myself. The only solution to finding real healing—the kind that mends even the cracks in our bones. The truth that there was a Someone greater, who not only saw my messiness and embraced me, but died for my messiness, changed my entire perspective on life and heartache. The love of Jesus breathed life into me. I'm sure you've heard the phrase "ask Jesus into your heart," but for me it was more like allowing him to see and touch my very wounded, battered heart. He saw me—all of me—and called me his daughter.

Jesus has a bad reputation for going around striking "sinners"—nonvirgins, homosexuals, maybe even Democrats—with lightning bolts, but that's just ridiculous. It's not who he is. Have you heard the story of the woman in the Bible who was caught having sex with a man who wasn't her husband?

A group of religious leaders, all men, brought her before Jesus. It's fair to assume she was barely clothed or perhaps even naked. These men asked Jesus how they should punish her—because the law at the time required she be stoned . . . to death. Many of you know this story, but I think Christian culture has rewritten the ending to have Jesus say, "Yep. I can't believe how disgraceful you are! Go read your Bible every day, beg for my forgiveness, get a few years of perfection under your belt, and then we'll talk." But that isn't what happened.

Jesus didn't respond right away; instead, he started writing in the sand. The religious leaders continued to shake their heads and pester Jesus with questions. They reminded Jesus of how terribly rotten this woman was to ensure he was paying attention. But after a long silence, Jesus stood and said, "Let the one who has never sinned throw the first stone!" One by one, the men leave, and Jesus and the woman are alone. Think about this scene for a second. She's barely clothed, lying in the dirt before someone she fully expected to kill her. I bet she wasn't breathing.

"Where are your accusers? Didn't even one of them condemn you?" Jesus asked the shamed woman.

"No, Lord."

And Jesus said to her, "Neither do I. Go and sin no more."

The message of Christianity is not "be perfect, don't have sex, make good choices, OR ELSE"—quite the opposite. There are stories throughout the Bible of Jesus choosing liars, thieves, prostitutes, and even murderers, and giving them a second chance after they did it all wrong. Not because they deserved it or promised to do better, but because he can change people. They couldn't change themselves, but Jesus could. You can't fix yourself, but Jesus can. So this "be good or go to hell" is never what Jesus intended—the real message is there will be no good people in heaven, just beautiful broken men and women like you and me who are forgiven.

I think our bedrooms represent some of our greatest mistakes and our greatest sources of shame—whether because of a sexual decision we made, nights of crying our eyes out, or maybe hiding, not wanting to face another day of hopelessness. For the past several weeks, I've had this image burned into my mind. This picture of Jesus walking into your bedroom right now and telling you that no matter what you did last night, or the last five thousand nights, you can have a second chance—a second chance at finding a good man, a second chance at purity, a second chance at a life spilling over with joy. You have screwed up, like everyone else on the planet, but that's why Jesus is standing there, above your bed, reaching out his hand to give you mercy and grace and a new life.

Real Women, Messy Bedrooms, and Hope
In 140 Characters or Less

#RealMenDontText

The past is the best predictor of the future.
#RealMenDontText

If Mr. Right walked into the room right now, would he be drawn to you?
#RealMenDontText

Six areas to focus on before marriage: childhood wounds, unforgiveness, selfishness, porn, money, fantasy relationships.
#RealMenDontText

You can have a second chance at finding a good man, a second chance at purity, a second chance at a life spilling over with joy.
#RealMenDontText

Jesus is standing there—in the midst of your greatest mistakes—reaching out His hand to give you mercy, grace, and a new life.
#RealMenDontText

CHAPTER 14

Real Love

the story we didn't write

{ ruthie }

"Strike three. You're out!"

It started on a sweltering summer day in the middle of a childhood game of baseball. Michael, three years my senior, remembers me striking out repetitively; I don't remember much about him, except that when his gangly self was around, I felt safe. He's always had a calming presence about him. His sister, Jordan, and I are the same age, and we choreographed dances to Mariah Carey and begged to stay out past our bedtime. We spent afternoons in her basement whispering about the mystery of growing up, each dreaming about the day we'd get to shave our legs and wear a bra.

The Deans bought property from my grandfather in 1989 to build their first house on the end of a quaint little cul-de-sac in Atlanta, Georgia. I lived around the corner—approximately ninety-two seconds away if I ran with shoes (not that I timed myself or anything), on a street called Orchard Knob. It was a friendly neighborhood where most families walked their dogs after dinner, lingering in the street discussing sports practices and the loads of homework the schools sent home. During the summer all the neighborhood kids played baseball during the day and reconvened at dusk to play spotlight tag. I assuredly never hit the ball, but let it be known that I had a knack for finding good hiding spots and not being spotted by the flashlight. My gangly, tall husband did not.

In 1993, the whole neighborhood basked in the excitement surrounding what became known as "the blizzard of '93," which brought paralyzing snowstorms to the entire Eastern Seaboard in the middle of March. School was canceled for the week, and we lost our power for a day or so, which meant we got to eat all the melting ice cream out of our freezer. My grandparents had the best sledding hill in the neighborhood, so Michael and I remember flying down the hill on our trash can lids with all our friends; it was truly the best week of our childhood. I cried when the snow finally melted and Mom said we had to go back to school (Michael did, too—he just doesn't remember). Michael and I played in the same Georgia creek, hit the same baseballs, knew the same hiding spots, and built forts in the same woods.

Michael's compassion and tender heart set him apart from the other kids on the street. For instance, when he was three, he comforted his crying mom, who was exhausted from dealing with a one-year-old, and said, "It's okay, Mommy. I here." Who does that? When he was six, he told his hairdresser—and any of his friends who would listen—about Jesus. At twelve, he started praying for his future wife. Michael displayed deep character, compassion for others, and a desire to live for something greater than himself from the beginning.

When I was eleven, Michael's dad took a job in North Carolina, and the neighborhood was sad to see his family go. I didn't see the Deans or think about them for fourteen years. Little did I know that Michael and I were written into a deeper story. We would meet again.

{ michael }

It's my favorite aspect of our story that Ruthie and I knew each other as kids. I remember her curls bouncing as she ran up the street to play with my sister. She was quieter back then, but just as fiercely determined as she admittedly is today. On numerous occasions I remember her winding up in fistfights with boys. In the first grade Ruthie received a character trait award for "courage" because she showed herself to be a fighter—"a defender of the weak," the teacher noted. I love this about her. She stands up for what she believes is right, occasionally to a fault, and I help temper her when she gets too heated. Ruthie tempers my insensitivity by helping me see others' perspectives and helping me identify my deeper desires.

At the age of twelve I started praying for my future wife at the direction of an influential man in my life. In high school I took my commitment to preparing for marriage very seriously and started asking God if my girlfriend at the time was the right one for me. When God's answer was no, I took it in stride and continued to wait. High school was difficult because my friends started having sex and I was committed to waiting. Again, not because sex is terrible or God was trying to punish me, but because God's love had captured my heart, and the instruction was to wait . . . for better. I clung to this promise and continued to honor my commitment to save sex for my wife. In college I pursued a few different relationships, convinced God certainly wanted me married right after graduation. When a relationship ended just before my senior year, and then a couple more in my twenties, it was difficult to trust God's heart for me. Would I ever have a great love story? Was I ridiculous for holding out hope?

It's amazing to think back on all the times when I thought God had forgotten me because I couldn't imagine this great love story I'd dreamed about ever coming to fruition.

{ r }

Bad Love Stories

As you've probably caught on and are tired of hearing about, I've tried to write hundreds of love stories. I had some hard single years, and there were times when I fully believed I would never find love.

After I discovered God had a bigger story for me, I started trying to write better love stories. I swore off my old ways of dating and committed to dating only men who not only called themselves Christians, but actually showed signs that Jesus had changed their lives—i.e., to start with they were sober and were waiting for marriage to have sex. The only problem was I kept trying to force the relationships and would become unraveled when they didn't work out. I matured over the years, but continued to attempt great love stories—to no avail.

Despite the many years Michael and I spent trying to figure out love on our own, we believe God was orchestrating a plan for us to fall in love. We laugh about how we never would have dated if we had met up again at any other time in our lives. I was the girl in high school he probably would have prayed for (ahem) and the freshman in college he would have avoided. He wouldn't have been "my type" until later in college—I would not have been instantly attracted to him had we met sooner. Timing really is everything.

At our engagement party, Michael gave a toast and said simply this:

> Many of you are not married, and I know it's hard to watch others enter a stage of life you long for. If I've learned anything over my twenty-nine years as a single man, it's that I can't write a good love story. It was only when I stopped trying to craft my own love story that I met my beautiful soon-to-be bride, Ruthie. My challenge to you is to let God write your story.

Not in a Box, Not with a Fox

My senior year of college, a friend convinced me to go on a mission trip to China, a humorous proposition considering I told God I would never, not in a box, not with a fox, not here or there or anywhere, become a missionary. Remember? I didn't even want to be a Christian at first. And a missionary was completely out of the question . . . or so I thought. I'm not sure what happened, but before I knew it, I was signing on the dotted lines of a visa application.

When I stepped off the plane in China, it was far from love at first sight—I don't like crowds, rice, or dirty bathrooms, and I get very motion sick on buses. All perfectly good reasons for me to leave China behind and never return. Around this time, Michael was living in Germany working for Young Life— where he spent five formative but lonely years in his twenties wondering if he'd ever have a great love story of his own.

A few years later I came to a crossroads with my career path. I had no clue what to do with my life, but since I like studying, negotiating, and—if we're being honest—designer clothes, I thought law school sounded like a great idea. I commenced studying and took several practice LSATs in my living room. I believed my scores meant God wanted me to be a lawyer.

After months of imagining what type of lawyer I'd become, I finally sat on my couch, surrounded by study guides, and asked God if he had any opinion on the situation. It only took about five minutes of silence before I had my answer. He wanted me to move to China. Trust me, I asked him if he was sure. You don't want to misunderstand an eight-thousand-mile move. He didn't speak in an audible voice; it was more of a gut feeling that I couldn't ignore. Walking away from the opportunity to become a lawyer was one of my most life-shaping decisions. Despite all the concerned looks I received from friends when I told them about my ever-so-slight change in direction, I was flooded with peace because I felt assured there was a plan bigger than I was, even if I didn't have all the details mapped out. As it turned out, I did like green eggs and ham after all.

If I had gone to law school, I wouldn't be a writer, for I first embraced my call to write while walking the bustling streets of China. If Michael had settled for the several nice girls he had dated along the way because he was tired of waiting, by the time I was ready to meet him, it would have been too late. God orchestrated something better for us.

{ m }

The Setup

While I was home from Germany one summer, my dad and I took a trip to Atlanta to visit friends from our old neighborhood. We went to visit Beth and David, and after a few minutes of catching up, Beth jumped off the counter and said, "You HAVE to meet Ruthie Harper." She later explained she had this overwhelming sense that she was supposed to re-introduce Ruthie and me, which she attributed to God.

Beth was a prayer partner for both Ruthie and me in our overseas ministries. She had been reading our newsletters and praying for us separately. Little did she know that she would play matchmaker!

Beth went on to describe Ruthie, and the part about China coupled with her description of a gorgeous runner piqued my interest. I had given up on trying to write my own love story and was really okay with being single. Instead of feeling stressed about dating and finding "The One," my motto became, "I can have coffee with anyone." I was content, even though I still wanted to meet Mrs. Right.

Due to some missed messages and wrong phone numbers, Ruthie never got word to call Beth back. I was hoping to meet her while I was in Atlanta (she was home from China for a brief stint), and I even ran by her house several times. Our last night in town, I confessed to my dad how bummed I was I didn't get to meet Ruthie.

Two days later, Beth finally got in touch with Ruthie and gave me her phone number. The funny part is Ruthie almost didn't give it to her because she wasn't open to being set up—but acquiesced because she really valued Beth's friendship. The rest is history.

{ r }

4,500 Miles

August 11, 2009

It was, as they say, the first day of the rest of our lives.

I was home from China for a brief period, on a Greyhound bus headed to Nashville. I looked down at the tiny little "1" on my phone screen, notifying me of a voicemail. I decided to listen to the message again before I deleted it:

"Hi, Ruthie. Beth gave me your number . . . and I was just calling to catch up. Sorry I missed you. . . . I'll try you again tomorrow."

His deep voice sounded reassuring, almost enigmatic, but I wasn't too keen on being set up with someone who lived in a different country. I was weary of men, having reverted to my high school thought pattern that marriage wasn't for me. I didn't plan on calling him back. After all, I was headed back to my home of honking taxis and crowded bathhouses in less than three weeks.

The bus pulled into Nashville, the sun gleaming off the surface of what the locals affectionately call "the Batman Building." Thankful to be off the bus that smelled like Chinese food doused in air freshener, I deleted the message. My friend picked me up, and I didn't think about Michael the rest of the evening.

The next morning I sat down and wrote in my journal—the same types of prayers I'd written over the past nine months. I prayed for healing, for perseverance. I asked God to show me how to love people more deeply and more fully. I closed my journal believing I'd entered another ordinary day. But I was so wrong.

For reasons beyond what I can put into words, I called the number of the man who I "probably have zero in common with." He answered, and we talked about living overseas, his cousin's upcoming wedding, what sports we played in high school, and of course, our old neighborhood. The conversation ended with the promise of another. We lived more than 4,500 miles apart from each other, much farther than ninety-two seconds with shoes. The stage was set for an impossible love story.

Keep Me Updated?!

After Michael and I headed back overseas, the "keep me updated" message landed in my in-box. In case you're curious,

I did not put him on my newsletter list or decide I would send him personal monthly updates. I was at a point in my life where my heart could not take another ounce of disappointment, and I remember praying, *God—let's make a deal. No more heartbreak. Deal?* I remember saying to the computer screen, "I am a great girl, and you are going to have to try harder if you want me" as I typed a very gracious but straightforward message:

"Hi, Michael! I hope you had a safe flight back to Germany. I enjoyed our conversations too! If you want to continue to get to know me, please call me. I'd love to hear from you!"

My friends are honestly the best a girl could ask for, because after the emergency e-mail concerning Michael's "keep me updated" message hit their in-boxes, everyone responded with kind messages about his intentions. But after a few dozen more days of long e-mail chains analyzing every punctuation mark, the "you're so hot, he's probably intimidated" explanation for Michael's message seemed less and less plausible—and most of my friends honestly told me they didn't think there was potential. I didn't breathe for two days waiting for him to respond. He was just perfect. Everything I wanted in a man—plus, he wasn't just tall, he was six foot four and had "puffy dark hair." This Michael Dean was very kind and made me laugh. He worked with kids. I remember telling God if he introduced me to "the perfect guy" only to not let it work out, I wouldn't speak to him for a while.

Regardless of all of Michael's perfectness, I wanted to take care of myself. I didn't want to sit around waiting for him to make a move, allowing him to string me along until he found someone better or lost interest. I didn't want to "play it cool," because in my experience playing it cool usually left me with a carton of ice cream in my lap, shouting about how rotten men are. I had standards for myself and needed to figure out sooner rather than later what kind of interest Michael had in me.

I was riding my bike down a familiar street in China when my phone rang. *Finally!* I thought, swerving precariously close to an overzealous taxi driver, who hopped the sidewalk as I (very smoothly, mind you) said, "Hello." *Michael Dean called me!* I tried to sound cool, collected, and not desperate—the opposite of what I felt. In reality, I came down with what I like to call "the nervous shakes and sweats," and my life was in danger as hundreds of bikers, cars, irritated bus drivers, and rickshaws whizzed by, all rolling their eyes in unison at the wobbly American who hadn't quite mastered the art of multitasking. Michael and I talked for two hours.

After two months or so of talking and getting to know each other, Michael stole my heart. I fell for him headfirst. I was fearful—petrified, really—of being hurt again, but that didn't stop my dreams of big bouquets of peonies and dancing under the stars. Our relationship was not a smooth ride from that point forward, because like any couple, we hit bumps and even roadblocks. At the beginning, I had to give myself pep talks and pore over relationship books, prying sticky little fingers away from my phone and keyboard. Daily. I wanted to control the relationship, to make it into what I wanted. But I had to trust that if he stopped calling or decided there was no "us," then I would save myself months if not years of my life where I could be with someone else. But Michael kept calling.

{ m }

Allow me to explain the "keep me updated" message. In a way, I was trying to play it cool, while attempting to protect myself from more relational hurt. Having recently gone through a breakup, I wasn't in a place to start dating again—but was surprised how much I was drawn to Ruthie. The breakup had nearly wrecked me, and I felt guilty about ending the relationship. I didn't understand why I hadn't found "The One" yet—most of us have those moments when it seems our time will never come. I sat down to journal and pray, as I did most mornings, and on a whim wrote a letter to my future wife. A letter I would give Ruthie when I proposed.

Sweetness of my heart,

I am waiting for you and have been praying for you since I was twelve years old. Waiting for you has been one of the hardest things I have ever done, if not the hardest. I cannot wait to start my life with you. I'm not sure if I know you yet or not, but it has been my prayer that when you come along, God would make it abundantly clear who you are. I want you to know that my breakup with her was in essence saying yes to you. I

*will wait for you as long as it takes. My heart is longing
to be with yours. I cannot wait to start a family with
you and go through the ups and downs of life with you,
my best friend. The past six months have been especially
hard; I did not realize how much of a sacrifice it would
be coming to Germany . . . the loneliness is unbearable
at times. My heart longs for the Lord and longs for
you. I will wait upon the Lord, who is worthy of our
praise, and in his strength be patient. I will continue to
pray for your protection, purity, and relationship with
God. May we pursue him as individuals with all of our
hearts until he brings us together. I love you!*

Michael

Ruthie's authenticity put me at ease, and I couldn't stop calling her. I could be myself with her on the phone (i.e., the online dating admission) partially because I felt I had nothing to lose, but mostly because of her accepting, kind spirit. She would tell me stories about visiting old ladies in China, bringing them bags of food, or dancing with the women in the town square, and I fell in love with her heart for people and lack of fear about unknown people and places. I remember that once she told me she was in a Chinese farming town sleeping in a room with chickens. What a woman! She wasn't afraid to be exactly who she was; I knew she would be an amazing wife and mother.

One phone call changed the trajectory of our lives. We made many, many mistakes and stumbled our way through a long-distance relationship, both wondering if this could possibly work. But the most important aspect was that while Ruthie and I were both coming from a place of hurt and cynicism about relationships, we were letting God write the story. Fully convinced that we couldn't write even the beginning of a great love narrative, we watched as our dreams, plans, passions, and desires united to embrace love. All the details—our foreign homes, our childhood, our love for Jesus—together crafted a beautiful love story.

{ r }

Down the Aisle

I stood behind the closed French doors, the sweet notes of "Amazing Grace" telling me it was almost time. The wedding planner fluffed my satin dress and veil. Breathe, I told myself.

The doors opened, and I knew the guests stood, the harp and violin grew louder, and the hot June breeze swept through the backyard. But all I saw was him. My groom. He waited for me at the end of the aisle—tears welling up in his eyes—as he watched me make my way down the stone steps toward him.

I can't believe he chose me. I can't believe he chose me.

I cried, even though I'd promised myself I wouldn't ruin my makeup. I was in disbelief that despite everything, Michael Dean chose me to be his wife.

It was a feeling I'll never fully be able to describe. Hundreds of eyes were on me, but I only saw him. Michael knew the darkest places in my life, yet he chose me. The thought beckoned a deeper realization that Jesus chose you and me, despite our shortcomings or promises to "get it right." He accepts us, bad relationship choices and all.

Marriage isn't easy. In between the rich companionship and exhilarating moments of intimacy are busy work days where we barely see each other, chores, arguments, budgets, and sacrifices to save for a home. A relationship takes work—because it isn't natural to give that much of yourself to one person.

Michael's loving me and choosing me daily are unlike anything I've ever experienced. He knows me fully and loves me completely. It is incredible to be known in such an intimate way. Our relationship with our spouse echoes the cry of an eternal God who chooses us, despite the dark areas in our lives.

Despite my mistakes and years of dating the wrong men, that moment our eyes met championed the significance of changing my relational decisions. What if I was still hopping from one guy to the next? What if I continued to let the bartender or the drug dealer or the burrito man drag me along? What if I was still analyzing text messages and weighing the pros and cons of meeting a guy last minute? I would have missed everything. Michael and I wrote this book because we want you, too, to know there's a better way to find what you're really looking for.

In the words of Joy Williams of the Civil Wars, "The longer you know someone—and the longer you allow someone to know you—the more the light and shadows inside each person become vivid." It is a dangerous process of knowing and being known, but the most beautiful, life-giving journey on which you will ever venture. It's never worth throwing away the best chapters of your life because you long to be with someone right now. Sometimes you just have to sit back and trust that soon enough your love story will take center stage—because chances are, there's a lot of writing happening behind the scenes.

About the Authors

RUTHIE AND MICHAEL DEAN grew up down the street from each other, but not being fans of convenience, they fell in love long-distance while Ruthie lived in China and Michael in Germany. Now happily married, the Deans love to run and take advantage of Sunday coffee dates (without technology), and they can often be spotted driving around Nashville in Michael's classic Ford truck. You can learn more about Ruthie and Michael and share your own stories of dating, love, and romance on Ruthie's blog, www.ruthiedean .com, or on Twitter @Ruthie_Dean or @MichaelDean10.

Ruthie and Michael would love to meet you on Ruthie's blog.

Join them at www.ruthiedean.com to read articles on life and dating and to share your own stories of love and relationships.

For discussion questions, visit www.realmendonttext.com to download for free.

CP0680